The Patriot Jihadi

The Memoirs of Shawn Pardazi

A Child Soldier's Transformation to A Patriot Guardian

Shawn Pardazi

with

Bahar Jahandideh

Contents

Foreword — vii
Bahar Jahandideh

Preface — xi

1. Wait, What? — 1
2. The Alamo — 8
3. Si O Se Pol — 16
4. Molotov Cocktail — 30
5. The Master – Al-Sayyid — 45
6. Kaboom — 53
7. Traditions and Honor Killings — 62
8. Muezzin — 70
9. The Escape — 75
10. Hard Landing — 82
11. No Judging — 87
12. The Blue Line — 91
13. Blondie — 97
14. You're FIRED! — 101
15. The Move It Is — 110
16. Stages of Jihad — 136

About the Author — 141
Also by Shawn Pardazi — 143

For more information, visit http://www.MyLETraining.com.

Cover Design by Shawn Pardazi

Photography by Shawn Pardazi

ISBN (print) 979-8-218-23225-2

ISBN (ebook) 979-8-218-23226-9

Library of Congress Control Number: 2023912685

This book is dedicated to my mother, who sacrificed her entire being to afford me the ability to seek refuge in the greatest country in the world while she stayed behind, suffering each day. Through her sacrifices, I can live in a place where freedom is paramount, and one can achieve their dreams. Thank You, Mom!
I wish I could see and hug you again!!

Foreword
Bahar Jahandideh

Some of you may have learned about Shawn Pardazi from someone you know or through his online platforms. Others may have attended his trainings or seen him on television. Or, you may have picked up this book, having never heard of him before. I'm a civilian with government consulting experience and plenty of knowledge regarding the Middle East, but I believe you will be as surprised and intrigued as I was by his story, regardless of your personal or professional background.

As a full-blooded Iranian, born and raised in the United States by parents who left Iran before the Revolution of 1979, even I was intrigued by various points throughout Shawn's story. My parents didn't have to escape. They didn't experience forced indoctrination and religious propaganda. It was difficult for me to imagine his circumstances and emotions as we moved through his story. I've never been a foreigner in a new land. The conveniences and security of living in the good ol' United States have always been a comfortable privilege for me, as I'm sure it is for many of you readers. My family's story differed greatly from Shawn's, yet we share many common facets of our personalities. Learning from Shawn's story has given me a deeper sense of pride in our Iranian culture. It has also deepened my love for this country of mine, the United States. We both feel a deep sense of patriotism for this land of the free and the foundation upon which this country was built.

Understanding everyone's mindset and background was necessary in every phase of Shawn's life. Before he even knew what it was called, he was observing, asking questions, and learning about people. For me to be able to write his story, I also needed to understand Shawn's background and mindset, as well as that of the key characters that made him into the man he is today.

Shawn is intense, passionate, and has a powerful personality with a diminutive stature. His self-deprecating humor regarding his height is balanced by the pride in his accomplishments and the legacy he is building for his young son. Spending several days of concentrated time getting the preliminary notes and outline covered taught me leaps and bounds about a man I thought I knew pretty well.

He was adamant that he needed to read his preface out loud to get back into his story mentally so that I could hear what he needed to convey beyond just the words on the page. As I sat and listened to him read, an energy shifted in the room. I heard him share his experience on 9/11, and when he paused, he was overwhelmed with emotion. I realized that the man who takes such pride in our culture and country of origin felt a sense of sadness and outrage at the events that occurred that day in America.

He would go on to have several moments of pause as he began to relive those moments in time again. He shared about leaving Iran and his beloved mother, not knowing if he would see either of them ever again. I recalled a conversation I had with my son earlier that day. (Interestingly, he's currently around the same age Shawn was when he left Iran.) My son said it felt like the longest week ever, even though I had only been away from home for three days. I thought about what I would have felt if I was Shawn's mother, sending my child to a land far away to keep him alive. I thought about how my son would feel being in Shawn's position, leaving everything he knew behind for a new world of unknowns. The truth is, we're all human. We have all been through circumstances that have shaped us and moved us. Things that pushed us to create new dreams and a new path. Along the way, we've met people that we struggled to understand. We hear things on the news or read something that makes us wonder, "Why?" or "How?"

Just as I have learned more about my own culture through listening to this story, I'm certain you, as the reader, will learn more than you expected. Shawn's vast knowledge of not just Iranian culture but other Middle Eastern countries, languages, and religions will blow your mind as you begin to understand how so many individuals around the globe think and operate. Shawn is a huge proponent of learning and sharing what he knows with others.

The backgrounds, motivations, and mindsets of individuals from this region can impact how they move, work, and, yes, even commit acts of terrorism around the world. There are also many who love their motherland while fighting for the safety and integrity of this homeland called the United States. To better understand, whether you work for a government or law enforcement agency or are a civilian like me, I encourage you to keep this book in a safe spot on your shelf because you'll reach for it many times for reference. There are keywords that will be explained and notable historical or cultural events that will continue to impact international relations globally.

I know this story will open your mind and heart as it did for me.

To Shawn, thank you for putting your faith in me and allowing me the honor of helping you share your story.

Preface

There are many assumptions regarding Muslims, especially regarding the circumstances surrounding 9/11 and other terrorist attacks around the world. To understand a terrorist's logic and motives is to understand the contributing factors to avoid lives being lost. It is important for you to learn and understand the logic and strategies behind the indoctrination of individuals abroad and here in the United States. Some government agencies will utilize this information to train their people, while civilians who are simply curious will learn about the people of the Middle East and their culture. The information in this book will also address some common misunderstandings. While some folks will attempt to cherry-pick information in this book to promote certain agendas, rest assured that my goal is simply to relay facts and my personal experiences; nothing more, nothing less.

Being a law enforcement officer has its challenges, but being a Muslim law enforcement officer in the Southern states is an entirely different challenge. Imagine coming to a new country where you can finally breathe a sigh of relief, knowing you'll be safe, a place where you can pursue your dreams and be anyone you want to be. But in the process of achieving your dreams, a small group of cowards attacks your new country in the name of "your" religion that they've hijacked. Imagine being a "good guy," but overnight, you become a "terrorist."

I love my country, family, and friends who have helped me become the man I am today. I love Iran, my homeland too. I bet you thought I meant Iran first, didn't you? Nope, I meant the United States of America. It's my country, my home, and it has been since I came here just before the age of fifteen.

This is a memoir of my life. It is my story of growing up in the early 1970s in a modern Middle Eastern country that rapidly changed to a theocratic regime, where religion dictated our every move. It was a country where elementary schools became training facilities for child soldiers. It was a country where theological studies were forced upon kids, and hatred towards Western society became deeply embedded in the new curriculum. I want to share my story because I hope that you will gain a better understanding of not only my personal background and how I became one of the top educators in my field but also the mentality of others who grew up in the Middle East and emigrated to countries around the world.

Imagine a child attending school, being indoctrinated to hate Western cultures and religions, such as Christians and Jews, and being forced to learn urban guerrilla warfare tactics by militants posing as teachers. I was that child! In 1979, while in the first grade, the Iranian Autocratic Monarchy of Reza Shah Pahlavi was overthrown by an Islamic Revolution. Such revolution came with immediate and forceful changes that impacted every aspect of life.

Overnight, every single law changed to reflect the extreme interpretations of Islamic principles as the country fell into the hands of Islamic Jurists. My school became a religious Madrasa (a religious school). Actually, all schools became that way. The local police were abolished, and many officers were killed since they worked for the Shah's regime. The police force was replaced with local fanatics, who embedded themselves in every aspect of local government in the name of Islam.

Our school day was converted to half a day of religious studies and half a day of military tactics. I became a child soldier recruit. Children either participated or their family was punished, some by hanging. This was the new Islamic Republic of Iran. In April of 1979, many of Iran's young population voted by referendum to write a theocratic-republican constitution, which triggered the beginning of the most devastating times in Iran.

This became known in Iran as the "Enqelab-e Eslami," or what we know as the Islamic Revolution. A revolution that made the country weak as it lacked military power. Two years later, Iraq invaded Iran, and as a 2nd grader, I was now being prepared for war. I was to be the next Shaheed (Martyr).

In this book, I will detail the process I went through as a child, becoming indoctrinated into militant Islam by the newly formed "Sepah-e Pasdaran-e Enqelab-e Eslami." It translates to "Islamic Revolutionary Guards Corps." Sepah, as I know it, are the "guardians" of the revolution in Iran. They sent representatives, as well as their militia members, which we call "Basij," to our schools to begin training the students to become "martyrs" for Islam. They were accompanied by Arabs, which I learned were Lebanese soldiers of what we all know as "Hezbollah" (The Army of God).

As an eight-year-old, I was confused but intrigued at the same time. We all know that at that age, every child is exploring idols and beginning to resonate in some form or fashion with a superhero. And they were made out to be superheroes, no doubt.

As this process started, within a year and a half, we heard the news that Iraq had invaded the Iranian cities close to the border and that we (the child soldiers of God) were going to help the Army defeat them. The Basij, Hezbollah, and Sepah ramped up their training regiments, and the entire male student population of my elementary school was now going out to the closest military base and training in military-style uniforms learning how to shoot Uzis and Machine Guns.

Of course, this came to a halt for me right before I turned fifteen when Basij and Sepah would come to the school and hurdle all those who had just turned fifteen on a military bus, and off to the border they went. My mother, who had been educating me behind the scenes about the difference between Islam as a religion and a political ideology, had made plans to send me to the United States.

My father lived in the United States, as both my parents had migrated to the USA in the late 60s, where I was born in San

Antonio, Texas, a few years later. However, I returned to Iran with my mother when I was a toddler. Being born in the United States meant I was a US Citizen, so through some coordination, I was able to fly to Turkey and get my American passport from the embassy in Ankara, and landed in Atlanta, Georgia, in early 1987. What a huge culture change, not to mention I didn't know how to speak the language.

As I grew up in the South, the first place being Alabama, I saw firsthand that the Christians I had heard so much about weren't what they were portrayed as. My stepmother Sue (God rest her soul), was the daughter of a preacher and one of the kindest souls I ever met.

Fast-forwarding a bit, I moved to Houston, Texas, at the age of sixteen to live with my uncle (mother's brother, Hassan). After navigating high school in my new country and learning to communicate in English, I decided to join Law Enforcement.

That was my calling. My purpose, and I knew it.

I climbed the ladder of success and was well on my way to becoming well-versed in the field of Counter-Smuggling, when the September 11th attacks changed my life forever. I found myself defending my religion to my peers while trying to find ways to do my part in protecting the land that I love.

My Country! My Home!

As I go through this book, I want you, as the reader, to take several things away. These include the fact that my religion also has fanatics that use it for their own political agenda. I will share the process of child soldier indoctrination and how understanding the mindset from the inside has helped me in various investigations in identifying potential threats to the homeland. I will provide reality versus fallacy, religion versus politics, and details of the trials and tribulations I have experienced in my 27 years serving the citizens of the United States. I served with the FBI, Homeland Security Investigations, Internal Revenue Service, and other specialized Task Forces that conduct investigations and intelligence collection on transnational organized criminal and terrorist enterprises.

Due to the nature of some of the investigations and intelligence collection encounters, I will not disclose exact locations nor real names of suspects, but rather the process and events that took place to help you get a glimpse of what it's like inside the mind of an extremist.

In addition, I will share some of the challenges I faced after 9/11 as it relates to my own peers and their reactions to my faith. It is my hope to allow the American public to know that, as American Muslims, we contribute to the United States in many aspects, including national security, and we also hate the terrorists who have hijacked our religion for their own political agendas.

Chapter 1
Wait, What?

At 8:03 AM central time on September 11th, 2001, my Motorola Razr V3 cell phone rang–I ignored the call. I was fast asleep as I had just arrived home around 7:30 AM from working the night shift at the Sheriff's Office. I worked as a Deputy Sheriff in the piney woods of deep East Texas. Not even ten seconds later, the phone rang again and again, I silenced it. It was the newest phone at the time and fit perfectly in my uniform pocket, but I was ready to throw it out the window.

About twenty seconds later, my phone rang again. This time I was really pissed off, as I had been asleep for less than an hour. I grabbed the phone and yelled, "Hello." I heard a cracking voice on the other side of the phone, sounding a little panicked but firm. It was my commander. He sniffled like he had a cold, but I had just left work two hours ago, and he didn't appear sick. I then realized he was tearing up.

I felt bad for yelling at him. He rambled off a few sentences but I wasn't fully awake, so it took me a bit to realize what he was saying. At first, I was still trying to gain my composure. I wasn't all there until I heard the words, "We're under attack." I assumed he was talking about someone attacking the day shift deputies, so I rolled off the bed and onto my feet, and started to pace toward the living room. The sound of blood rushing through my head was clearly audible in my ears and I felt my ears getting hot. My heart rate was probably over 160 BPM. I walked into the kitchen of my small one-bedroom apartment about forty miles from work, trying to wrap my head around what he was rambling about. The signal of my GSM phone was cutting in and out, which didn't help the matter much. I then heard him say, "We're under attack. Someone crashed a plane into the Twin Towers in New York City. It's all over the news. Stay by your phone and be ready to respond if we need personnel."

I grabbed a bottle of water from the refrigerator and rummaged through the living room area, looking for the television remote. I was distraught, still half asleep, and high on adrenaline. I finally found the remote control and turned on the TV. I usually watched the news when I woke up to stay in tune with national affairs, and CNN was the channel it was set on.

The first thing I saw was live footage of the smoke smoldering out of one of the twin towers. Within a minute or so, as I was grabbing my uniforms and getting my duty gear in order in case I was called out, I watched the second tower being hit by another plane. I stopped dead in my tracks. I could not believe my eyes. The fiery explosion when the plane hit the second tower brought back flashbacks. Flashbacks of when I lived in Iran and the Iraqi MIGs would attack our city. I had seen similar carnage before.

I remember walking home from school when I was about ten years old, sirens ringing throughout Esfahan, where I grew up. Within a minute, I saw and heard the Iraqi MIGs diving down in the open blue skies, and I saw the air-to-surface missiles shooting from their wings. I followed one as it was going to my right and watched it hit a ten-story building about two blocks from my school. It was the building that housed the Basij office.

The sound and flash of the explosion, followed by the smoke, looked just like the footage I was watching on TV. I felt a chill hit me, and it felt like a ton of bricks. I was in total shock. I felt like I was back home and could recall the exact emotions. They were a combination of fear, anger, and helplessness that overcomes a person's mind and soul as one sees pure carnage unfold in front of their eyes.

To put things into perspective, consider the emotions you would feel if you witnessed a horrible vehicle crash directly in front of you; a scene where you hear the sounds, feel the force of the crash and subsequently freeze in your steps. This is usually followed by the urge to help, but unlike an accident scene, during an attack, there's still the possibility of a secondary attack or explosion.

As I stood there in shock and watched the television screen, I felt the fear start to dissipate, but as it did, anger took over. I remember screaming the word "FUCK" at the top of my lungs and saying, "I'm going kill those mother fuckers." Knowing I was more than 1500 miles from the scene and had no clue who the hell was doing this still didn't seem to affect or change my opinion. I was out for blood now. I was pissed. How could someone or a group attack the people just now going to work? Are we being attacked by another country? Are these people going to attack other cities? Questions like this were flooding my brain.

I was glued to the TV, standing in the living room in my underwear, holding a bottle of unopened water. As I flipped the channels to see what other information was being disseminated, I heard another plane had crashed into the Pentagon. Another reporter said, "Anonymous Sources are saying that this is potentially an orchestrated attack by Islamic Terrorists." At that moment, I lost it. I threw the remote against the wall, slammed the water bottle on the coffee table, and shattered the glass top. I didn't even realize what had happened.

The sheer anger I felt when I heard the term "Islamic Terrorists" was so deep that if I had been face to face with one of those animals, I would have slaughtered them with my bare hands. This is NOT the Islam I know. These people are NOT Muslims, I kept saying in my head. I sat down on the couch, muted the TV, and stared at the floor. I was so angry; I didn't even realize I had walked on the broken glass, and my right middle toe was bleeding with a shard of glass protruding out of it. I never felt it. I grabbed the shard and pulled it out. Never felt the pain. I went to the bathtub and attempted to wash off the blood to bandage it up. I knew it would be a matter of time before I would get called out again.

I sat down, regained my composure, and swept and vacuumed the glass off the floor over the next thirty minutes. I had shattered the remote but luckily had an extra universal remote in my bedroom. As I sat back down and unmuted the TV, I started to flip through the channels. I saw more footage of the carnage. By this time, the flight that had crashed in the Pennsylvania field was being shown. I thought about all the innocent lives taken—all of the innocent passengers and the people in those buildings.

I didn't get called in that day, but I was wide awake. I monitored the news channels, and the more details that emerged, the more pissed off I became. It was a roller coaster of emotions, especially when I heard that the attacks were most likely orchestrated and delivered by followers of Osama Bin Ladin and declared by him as a Jihad Against America. The news said that these were suicide missions by terrorist operatives.

I began to realize the American populous was probably trying to not only find out why this was happening but also what would drive someone to commit suicide for a cause. I knew the process firsthand. I experienced the process of indoctrination. I knew it would be a matter of time before my co-workers and those who knew I was Middle Easterner would start asking questions. So, I had to reach deep inside to gather my thoughts to explain to those around me the process and what contributes to the mindset.

How was I supposed to help the American people understand that the value of life is not the same when one is indoctrinated and brainwashed overseas? Having attended high school in the US, I knew that religious topics were not part of the curriculum unless one chose to take certain courses during the last two years. These topics were usually reserved for undergraduate studies and onward.

I remember being in Iran and sitting in class with a cleric, a Pasdari (IRGC Soldier), and listening to him tell us that our lives on this Earth are only to serve Allah and that there is no greater reward but to die for the cause of Allah. He justified the revolution in Iran and the implementation of Islamic rules as a Godly act, and the purpose was to push out the "Great Satan," referring to the United States. He called the Shah of Iran a puppet for the West and the Jews, and since the West was following Christianity and Jews were traitors of Prophet Mohammad, who tried to get the Prophet Mohammad killed, they were both representatives of Shaytan (Satan).

These types of lectures and sermons, using religious texts from the Quran, were always mentioned and reinforced by mentioning hadiths. I will cover these in later chapters and how they are cherry-picked to serve a purpose or even totally interpreted wrongly to promote an agenda.

At many of the mandatory lectures, we were told that we were soldiers of Allah and that upon being trained, we would be the "Army of God" (aka Hezbollah). So, in essence, we would be fighting for the cause of Allah, and if we died doing so, we would go straight to heaven since our entire being is for the purpose of fighting for Allah.

In the process of these lectures, the value of human life is minimized, and emphasis is placed on the "work" done for the sake of religion. The reward for doing the soldier's work was guaranteed paradise in the afterlife, especially if the fight involved suicide and sacrificing oneself to hurt the enemies of Allah; hence, making suicide legitimate.

It had all clicked when I heard the attacks were suicide missions. I knew exactly where the mind of those responsible was. They didn't value the lives of anyone on those planes or inside those buildings, not even women and children. I knew all too well how they had been brainwashed.

But this was not my religion. I was lucky to have a grandfather who helped educate me in my early years. This is between the time I was three and seven years of age. He passed away due to an illness around the Revolution, so he wasn't alive to see the atrocities that followed.

He used to read the Quran to me and translate it into Farsi, explaining them in stories for me to understand. I remember him telling me that to grow up and be a good Muslim, one must do everything in their power to help the needy, protect the weak and serve God by serving mankind. "The killing of an innocent person is like killing the entire world," I remember him saying one day. This was because, at about five years old, I had some toy soldiers, and as I was playing with them in our enclosed yard, I acted as if I shot another toy that was a civilian. I vividly remember my grandfather walking over to me as I was seated on the tiled ground and asked me, "Why did you kill that man?" I responded with, 'I don't know, I just killed him." He replied, "Pesar (son in Farsi), never hurt anyone who is not aggressive towards you, and only take action when you have to in order to defend yourself or another who cannot defend himself." He continued by saying that the Prophet and the Quran forbid the killing of innocent persons and recited what I mentioned about the killing of all mankind.

Good thing I had teachers like my grandfather who had shown me some insight into the reality of the religion before I was forced to attend the brainwashing sessions at school. I can attest to the fact that the way these clerics are able to justify their ideology by manipulating the religious content is extremely easy, and those who have no solid foundation in the religion can easily be influenced.

Such was the case for those terrorists. I knew their mindset and why they committed the atrocities. They lived their lives for one cause, and no matter what, that was the only thing that mattered. In their mind, they were doing God's work. I don't know what "god" they are referring to, but that is not the God of Abraham.

Having relived my childhood and my experiences in those several hours following the attacks changed my focus. I knew I was going to be questioned, so I dove into more studies of my religion to have answers. After all, I was the only Middle Eastern and Muslim law enforcement officer in East Texas, and the questions would come eventually. I just didn't know that it would be for the next 21 years and I would also face other challenges and derogatory comments from those I served alongside.

Chapter 2
The Alamo

When I think of the Alamo, I think of Santa Anna's gruesome takeover during the Battle of the Alamo, where he slaughtered a lot of Texans and Tejanos. But, of course, his reign was over a couple of months later at the Battle of San Jacinto. Now, unless you're a true Texan, you don't know what I'm talking about, but that's okay. To this day, this historic building serves as an iconic landmark in San Antonio, Texas. It has a rich history, shown by the display of artifacts and memorabilia, and millions of visitors frequent the area annually.

So, what's the significance of the Alamo in my memoirs, you ask? It's pretty cut and dry. I was born in San Antonio, Texas! YES! That's correct. I'm a true Persian/Texan who didn't know a lick of the English language when I came back to the States in 1987. But, if you were to speak to me today or hear me at one of my seminars, you'd think my name is Jeremy Smith. Sometimes, when I call my bank or one of my credit card companies about an issue, I tell them my name, and there's a long pause. I know what they're thinking. They hear my accent, sounding like I'm farm raised from the piney woods of East Texas, and then look at my name.

The Patriot Jihadi

As you saw on the cover, the name I use is Shawn Pardazi. There's a reason for that, and we'll cover that later in the book. But what most don't know is that my whole name is Seyed Ibrahim Shaheen-e Moayedpardazi. I would write in Farsi here, but 99% of readers wouldn't know what it says. So just imagine what looks like chicken scratch, written from right to left, and leave it at that!

Now you can see the issue when I call a financial institution, attempting to discuss my accounts. The silence is always there. I must break that initial silence by saying, "I know, I don't sound like the name," chuckling, and telling them they can just call me 'Shawn." The sigh of relief follows instantaneously, and the tone quickly changes. I can't say I blame them, though. I'd be skeptical if I heard a name that long paired with a Texan accent.

My parents came to the United States in 1968. While my father was finishing his Medical Doctorate at the University of Texas in San Antonio, my mother was a nursing supervisor at the San Antonio Memorial Hospital. They had met in Iran at the University where they both pursued medical degrees. They married after completing their studies and decided to come to the land of the free and take part in the American motto of life, liberty, and the pursuit of happiness.

My mother had secured a position at the hospital, while my dad completed mandatory classes in preparation for the Medical Licensing Exam to practice in the States. He was already a medical doctor in Iran, but to practice in the States, he would need to pass the exam stateside.

Somewhere in the midst, they decided to have a kid, and I was brought into this world in jhe greatest land God ever created—the Great State of Texas. Having the State of Texas on your birth certificate is an honor. It is, in fact, the only state that can fly its flag at the same height as the flag of the United States. But, of course, only a Texan would understand the meaning behind what I'm referring to here. I'm pretty sure that my Texas drawl was set in at birth, which is why I confuse people when they hear me switch from a Texan to Mississippian to an Alabamian accent in the same conversation! Add in the element of my Middle Eastern name, and you have the perfect recipe for a brain scramble!

Since my name is so long and a tongue twister, they called me "Alphabet" in the Police Academy. I mean, when you have to stencil your whole last name on a t-shirt in three-inch letters, there isn't any room left anywhere on the fabric. So, I learned to just go by the name 'Shawn Pardazi.' Middle Easterners will adopt an American name, and we typically try to choose a name that is as close to our ethnic name, though I have known a Mohammad or Hassan that go by "Mike" or "Tony." You can blame American classics like 'The Godfather' or 'Scarface' for that. What can I say? Iranian men love a good Al Pacino flick!

Farsi is my first language because my mother's father needed care when I was still a baby, and she took me back to Iran to care for him. My father was establishing his medical career in Texas, so suffice it to say that it was not a great scenario for a long and happy marriage. They divorced, and I spent the next thirteen years in Iran with my mother, maternal grandfather, and later on, my stepfather, whom I referred to as "Amu" (paternal uncle). In Farsi, there isn't a word for "stepmother/stepfather," so Amu was the closest substitute. Interestingly, in Farsi, we differentiate between the maternal and paternal sides regarding aunts and uncles. It comes in handy when trying to keep certain relatives straight, although Farsi has a lot of words and phrases that leave you guessing until you hear the entire context!

My beloved grandfather comes to mind as I ponder my earliest memories in Iran. My mother's father was the earliest role model in teaching me about Islam, and he was a paternal influence in my life from an early age until my mother remarried. My time in Iran, attending school and mosque, allowed me to learn Arabic as well. It was encouraged that all children in

Iran learn Arabic to be able to read the Quran in its original language.

My mom and I lived with my grandfather, who became my father figure. He was a tall man with broad shoulders and a bald head. He had large dark rings around his eyes, thick and bushy salt and pepper brows, and a square jaw. If I didn't know better and saw him in the States, I would have thought he was German or Austrian. You know, those large-stature males who tower over everyone and just scare the shit out of you the way they look at you. My grandfather had those eyes-the dark-colored Persian eyes that penetrate your soul. You didn't even have to be questioned by him and would confess all your wrongdoings as he glared at you.

When I was about five years old, I ran into the kitchen area with mud on my shoes. I had been playing football (American Soccer) in the alleyway with friends, and it had rained the day before. So the old dusty alleyway had become a mud puddle. That was a no-no in my culture.

The floors of our home, including the kitchen, were always to be clean. What shoes are worn outside are taken off outside the door or inside and left at the foyer. No outside elements could be introduced into the house. In an Islamic home, the floors are also used to lay out the rugs to pray when it's that time of the day, so no forbidden articles are to be on the floor. Hence, a shoe smeared with mud was not allowed anywhere near the flooring. Most homes have open kitchens that lead to the living area and courtyard "hayyat," a central open-air space in the middle of many homes in Iran. You will often see this type of communal space in houses in North Africa, and many parts of the Middle East and the Mediterranean region. Most homes have tile floors and area rugs, but in our case, expensive Persian rugs are strewn in every room to decorate and provide a softer ground to walk on.

If a pair of slippers are worn in the home, they are to be

taken off as one enters the bathroom, where another pair of slippers is worn before entry. The same slippers a mom wears and throws when she's pissed at any of the family members. It's a sign of anger and disgust. An Iraqi journalist displayed the same type of act in December of 2008 when George W. Bush was subjected to the shoe throwing at his press conference with Nouri al-Maliki, Iraq's Prime Minister.

When I ran into the kitchen that fateful day, I took about three steps, and "SMACK" on my forehead was a pair of large-ass rubber slippers. There, implanted on my forehead was a huge red mark. I was stunned! I stopped dead in my tracks and looked as if Satan himself had attacked me. My grandfather was beaming right at me when I heard his deep voice tell me in Farsi, "Eh, Pedar Sag, boro biroon va kafsheta dar beyar." What he was saying was, "Hey, you. The one with a dog as a father, go outside and take your shoes off." It sounds funny now, and even translating the saying into English sounds funnier. But when it happened, I was shivering.

My grandfather was a good man, but he was your typical Persian grandpa. Middle Eastern men who grow up overseas have a personality about them. It's that ten-foot-tall and bullet-proof personality that demands respect and immediate compliance. And if compliance and apology are not returned, an ass-whooping is to follow. An ass-whooping that in the states would be considered extreme child abuse and a felony in most states. But overseas, it's part of the culture in every household. Calling the cops? Oh, hell no! You call the cops for some shit like that on your parents, and the cops come and whoop your ass in front of the parents while the parents cheer them on.

I saw this with my own eyes once when the kid two doors down from us ran to a Pasdari (Soldier of the IRGC) and complained his dad had whipped him. The Pasdari brought the kid back to his home and told the father what the kid had said. The father then told the soldier to take care of it. The soldier smacked the kid in the face, kicked him in his ass, and pushed him into the doorway of the home right into the arms of his mother. Well, she then slapped him again. The dad closed the door, and I could hear the kid screaming; his mother was slapping him around for taking household business outside the home. You just don't do that in our culture. This is primarily why Middle Eastern people are very private about their personal lives, and when abuse is present, no law enforcement is ever contacted stateside.

Iranian-style parenting is not for the weak at heart. Iranian parents and grandparents love with everything they have and then some. Emotions are intense. They don't just love a regular amount. They love you with their organs, or you become as dear to them as an organ. I know, I know - I might have lost you there! Persian sayings don't translate into English well, but to tell a loved one they are so very dear to you, just as your liver is necessary to your body, is considered an endearment and a very nice thing to say! Culturally, to discipline your child is to love them so much you don't want to see them make the same mistake again in the future. You want to protect the child but also teach the lesson in a way that hopefully never needs repeating.

As I grew older, I learned how to deal with certain ailments. I remember one night, my ear was hurting to the point that even the sound of someone else talking was making it hurt. My mother, the head administrator at one of the largest state hospitals, told me to see Baba Bozorg (That's Grand Dad in English). So, without missing a beat, I ran to my Baba Bozorg's room and knocked on the glass window panes. The doors in our old house were metal but had a large window pane in the center, usually covered with a small curtain with Persian artwork. My grandpa yelled, "Befarmaeen," which meant, "You're welcome to come in." I cracked the door a little to make sure he knew it was me before I barged into his room.

With a big ass smile, my grandpa motioned for me to come and sit with him. In his room, my grandpa had a seating area decorated with a nice Persian rug that was hand woven with wool, and around the rug, he had small pillows against the walls to sit Indian style and lean against the pillow. So, I sat on the wall adjacent to his right. My grandpa used to smoke opium. It was a common thing back in the day, during the Shah's regime. Now, I do have to clarify that he wasn't an addict. Opium use was like how Marijuana is used in the States. You have your hippies, high as a kite, and your bums, who just couch surf and smoke weed all day but don't have the long hair and the lolla-palooza tats. And then you have the business professionals who smoke just to take the stress off from a hard day's work. My grandpa was one of those. He had his two or three nights a week ritual and then would sit with us in the main living area and drink hot tea.

Chai is a type of hot tea and has been a main antiquity in Persian culture for thousands of years. The same goes for Afghans and Arabs. So as my grandpa was loading up the pipe to get that sizzling charcoal up and near the Taryak (opium paste) on top of the round porcelain end, he looked at me and asked if my ear hurt. I said, "Bale Baba Bozorg" (Yes, Grandpa). He said my mom had told him about it, and he would fix it. He then told me to get close to his side and took a big hit off the pipe exhaling a huge cloud of smoke. I thought the entire room was about to disappear. The man had lungs that could suck in every air molecule out of the room, leaving everyone else without oxygen.

I was sitting there, in awe of how much smoke he had just blown into the room when he hit me with his elbow and asked, 'Kodoom Gooshet Dard Mikoneh' (Translated: Which ear is hurting). I reach over and point to my left ear. Both were hurting, except the left one was hurting really bad. He takes a big hit off the pipe and turns over towards me, grabs me by the forehead and the back of the head, turns my head to where my left ear is facing towards him, and commences to blow the entire inhaled pool of smoke right into my ear.

The shit stunk, but within five seconds, the pain was gone! Just like that! There I was at the time, thinking my grandpa was a genius and a healer. It wasn't until I became a cop and a narcotics agent in the States that I realized that codeine and other painkillers are made from opium. Go figure; I was being treated with the actual plant and its natural effects, while stateside, one would pay up to $4000 for similar treatments at a hospital. Little did I know I would have to answer, "Have you ever ingested or taken any illegal drugs" on my law enforcement and national security position applications. Just imagine what went through my mind during my polygraph examinations. Since I wasn't smoking it, I never saw it as "using it," so when I said "No," the lie detector didn't detect any deception in my response. Plus, it probably helped that I even told myself that it might be illegal in the States, but it was fully legal in Iran, and the laws of the States don't regulate or apply to other countries. Maybe that helped me disassociate from the question and remove the contributing factors that show up on a lie detector test as deception. In my mind, I wasn't doing anything illegal at the time my grandpa blew that smoke in my ear. Just don't try this home remedy here in the U.S.A.!

Chapter 3
Si O Se Pol

"Si O Se Pol," meaning Thirty-Three Poles, is the name of one of many historical landmarks of Esfahan, Iran. I grew up in Esfahan, which is so rich in the old Persian culture that you can't go two blocks and not see a building that dates back thousands of years.

In late 1977, my mom introduced me to her new fiancé, who eventually became my stepdad. His name was Alireza. I remember him so vividly. He was a square-jawed man with broad shoulders and a perfect hairline that accompanied his stylish and full head of hair. He wore it slicked back like an Italian mobster, and he always dressed in a suit and tie. He drove a Paykan, an Iranian automobile, which was designed by designers from Britain and was viewed as the Chevrolet cars of Iran. We know that Chevy is the 'Heartbeat of America,' and Paykan was the same status as Chevy in Iran.

There's no substitute for the word "stepdad" in Iran that sounds respectable, so anyone who has a stepfather usually calls them "Amou." Amou, which has the literal meaning "uncle," is a general term a child would call an uncle from the father's side. The uncle from the mother's side is called a "Daii." This term sometimes extends to the husband of an aunt as well, along with just about any male figure who is related to the family unit through marriage. It's a term of respect, for sure.

On a Wednesday afternoon, Amou Reza came home from work and wanted to take me to eat "Chelo Kabob" (ground beef grilled on skewers, typically with grilled tomatoes and onions and served over rice or with bread.) This cultural cuisine has become a worldwide favorite. Many countries in the Mediterranean and the Middle East have their own version, altering the meat mixture with other proteins, spices, or accouterment served with the main meal. I've never seen an Iranian kid not love Chelo Kabob; it's one of the ultimate comfort foods. Chelo Kabob is the most known of Iranian dishes, almost as if it's the national food, kind of like Hot Dogs and Apple Pie is for the American culture. Or even Fajitas for the Mexican culture. If you've never tried Persian food, I suggest you do. You'll either love it or hate it. And no, just because a restaurant says Mediterranean food on the sign doesn't mean you're getting Persian food. Persians are very prideful of their culture and will have a mention of "Persian" in their restaurant name or description.

As we drove over to the restaurant owned by one of his friends, he told me he had to stop somewhere on the way. As we drove down Bahman Boulevard, nearing Shayan Street, he took a fast left on Shayan and sped up, appearing that he was running away from someone. I looked over at Amou and he was constantly checking the rearview mirror. He made three more turns and then pulled into an alley filled with stray cats roaming around dumpsters. I was a little shaken and couldn't say anything. I didn't know what was happening, but I had this sense that Amou Reza had seen someone and was trying to escape them.

I had no clue why, and I was too scared to ask. In our culture, you don't ask an elder "why" they do something as it can be a direct insult as if you are "questioning" them. It's an issue of respect, and kids just don't disrespect elders. Huge no-no! So, I just stared at his face as he was constantly glancing between mirrors and looking ahead at the next cross street that intersected the alley. I sat there, quiet as a mouse. And then I noticed his shoulders drop as he let out a deep sigh. He looked at me, smirked, and almost in a smart-ass way said, "Tarsidi?" (Scared you?). I was still shaken, and all I did was nod my head up and down. He burst out laughing and told me, "Bi Khiyal Amou Joon, na tars. Kesee bema kari nadareh." Basically, he said, "Don't worry about it; no one is after us."

I might have been only five, going on six, but I was no dummy. I could see his veins thumping in his neck and his brows scrunched down, but his eyes were wide open. The same way when someone is shocked and scared at the same time. But he played it off well. I didn't ask anything, but hell, I was just five; what was I supposed to ask? I was just glad we were going to eat. I love Chelo Kabob. And even now, when I travel to a big city in the States or Canada, the first thing I do is pull up Yelp and punch in 'Persian Food.' I can't kick the habit. It's in my blood, you could say.

As Amou Reza pulled out of the alleyway, we rode back streets for about four kilometers, and I had no clue where we were going. But it sure didn't appear to be anywhere that would have a "Kababi" (a kabob restaurant). We pulled into a dead-end street that was barely wide enough for the small sedan we were in, and Amou Reza drove about 400 meters before stopping directly in front of a door to a home. Unlike the West, the alleys and streets are where the front door of the homes are. Homes are all built next to each other, and the wall of the home is where the pavement or the concrete of the street starts. I saw metal reinforced doors that usually would be associated with a backdoor of a store at the mall in the west, but overseas it would be the entrance to someone's home.

As soon as he put the car in park and honked, the door

slowly creaked open, and I saw a man stick his head out and look up and down the alley before walking out to our car and kneeling over into the passenger window. When he bent over, towering over my head, I couldn't help but notice a pistol in his waistband. I had seen guns before, but only being carried by the Artesh (Army) and the Ajan (Police). To this point, I'd never seen a firearm on someone wearing regular "civilian" clothes. The man had a rough look on his face; his brows were thick, black, and bushy. He just had one of those faces that gives you the feeling that he was a bad person. He looked at me and smiled, but his smile was dry and cold. His posture scared me.

He told Amou Reza that he had the envelope and for us to drive around once and return. Here I am, five years old, supposed to be going to eat Chelo Kabob, and now going in circles with my stepdad and experiencing things I have no clue about; it was scary, and all I knew is that I was starving. I still didn't make a sound. Amou Reza threw the car in first gear, and off ahead we went. He turned left at the next alley and looked over at me; he was giggling, but I was confused and didn't know what to say. I probably had a look on my face that screamed, "Take me home." He raised his left hand and rubbed the top of my head, and threw around my thick hair, saying, "Pesaram, na tars. Manam hafteer daram" (My Son, don't be scared, I have a pistol too). I was locked in my place, and my eyes were about to bulge out of my head when he pushed aside the right side of his coat, and I saw a huge pistol in his waistband. I said to him, "Amou, chera to hafteer dari?" (Why do you have a pistol?). He said softly, "Man baraye dolat Shah car mikonam" (I work for Shah's government). Of course, at five years old, I had no clue what the hell he was saying and what a government was, but I knew he was a good guy, and I didn't have to be scared.

We made the block and went right back to the front door of the guy's house. The man came out, handed my stepdad an envelope, and we drove off. As we drove away, my stepdad took a paper money bill out of the envelope and handed it to me. It was 1,000,000 Rials. My eyes were fixated on the zeros. Even at a young age, I knew that was a lot of money, or it was back then, anyway. The Iranian Rial was valued a lot higher back in the Shah's regime in Iran since the US and UK were great allies of Iran.

All happy and giddy, we made a few turns as my stepdad whistled the national anthem of Iran (Shah's regime) and finally made it to the restaurant. This was the first time I had ever gone anywhere with my stepdad. He had married my mom about six months prior but was always traveling for work. I never knew what kind of work he did until much later in life. After he passed away some years later, by which time I was already in the States, I learned during the Shah's regime he was a SAVAK (Sazeman-e Ettelaat va Amnita-e Keshvar) Agent, which was the Iranian Secret Police and Intelligence Services for the Pahlavi Dynasty. And to my amazement, he was way up in the food chain too. I guess you could say I've grown up around "intelligence" and the "security" culture my entire life.

SAVAK: The secret police, domestic security, and intelligence agency in Iran during the reign of the Pahlavi dynasty. SAVAK operated from 1957 until prime minister Shapour Bakhtiar ordered its dissolution during the climax of the 1979 Iranian Revolution. At its peak, SAVAK had approximately 5,000 agents.

We found a parking place directly in front of the restaurant. In the States, most restaurants are in shopping centers or in a building of their own. But in Iran, at least at that time, all the stores were lined up in a row, and the only thing separating them from the asphalt of the street was a large sidewalk. Imagine walking out of the shopping center here, from any store, and as soon as you step off the sidewalk, there's just enough room for a car to parallel park and then the lanes of the boulevard. You could literally open your car door, and it could be taken out by a passing car. The funny thing is, I hardly ever saw a car crash. Folks in Iran knew how to drive!

As we walked into the restaurant, about half the restaurant stood up and greeted my stepdad. Now remember, I had no clue what he did at the time and had never been out with him, so what I thought at the time was "my stepdad" was a very popular man. That he was, no doubt! I later learned that this particular restaurant was kind of like the hang-out for the higher-ups of the Shah's government and mostly were secret police employees. But hell, at five years old, it was kind of status-building.

I talk about status, but someone who reads this probably wonders, "Why was he concerned with status as a five-year-old?" It's not overcompensation but rather a cultural attribute of Persians. As I said, Persians are very proud of their lineage, and the higher status someone has, the more respected they are in the community. Folks are called by their status. If someone is a Doctor (Any sort of Ph.D.), he or she is always called by the term "Doctor" first before their last name is mentioned. An example of this can be noticed by Americans who have Persian friends. You'll hear them speak of someone who is a relative or a friend, but they emphasize their education level. If a Persian was to introduce you to or speak of someone they know, they'd say their name and most definitely continue by saying something like, "and he's a Doctor of Oncology " as if that has anything to do with talking about someone who has a house for sale.

As we sat there, a male waiter came to the table and addressed my stepdad as "Sartip." I knew what that name was even at my age. Sartip was the rank of a Brigadier General in the Armed Forces of Iran at the time. As I mentioned, a person's status is always how they are called upon by others. When I heard this, I was proud. Why? My stepdad was a Brigadier

General. That's huge when it comes to status. I knew about the military ranks because, as a young boy growing up in any Middle Eastern country, the military is viewed as the elite who carry weapons, and any kid you know is going to be drawn to the soldier in a uniform, even in the States. You can't go to any toy store and not see toy soldiers and military-related toys. It is a male thing. It's universal. Every kid wants to be a badass soldier. Even my own son, Seyed Kamran, at six years old here in the States, tells everyone he wants to be a "Navy SEAL" when he grows up.

My stepdad ordered a Soltani plate for himself and me a Khoresht Gheime. He talked to a few people who kept coming to our table until our food arrived. We ate our food and got ready to leave when one of the men behind the counter called him to the front of the register area and handed him the store phone. My stepdad seemed to be in a rush, and after he quickly got off the phone told me to let's run to the car because he must go to work. He drove fast to the house, where he took me in and told my mom he had to go to Tehran for a few days. He grabbed his bag, which he always had packed, and he was gone. I didn't see him for another three weeks.

I asked my mom, "Maman, Amou Reza Che Kari Mikoneh?" which is "What kind of work does Uncle Reza do?" She looked at me and, with a soft nonchalant voice, said, "Namayand-e Foroosh'e Darooi," which means a "Pharmaceutical Sales Rep." I had no clue what that was and asked why he had to have a gun and that he had told me he worked for the Shah. My mom slapped me in the mouth so hard I felt the tingling behind my neck and a tear on my upper lip. I just stood there speechless and stunned. She lowered her voice, came about two centime ters from my face, and in a stern and angry-sounding quiet voice said to me that if I ever repeated what he had told me or mentioned it to anyone, she would beat me with a shovel. And man, let me tell you, that shit hurts.

Beatings are a part of normal culture. It's nothing like the states, where you have children's protective services and victim's services overseeing households. In Iran, really all of the Middle East, punishment of a child or a household member is a civil issue and not the business of authorities. The laws don't even protect kids. So, if you end up with psycho parents and they kill you, it is what it is, especially if the parents are well-educated and have money. I was lucky, though, neither my mom nor my stepdad were sickos. They whooped my ass when I acted stupid, thought I would make my own decisions, talked back, or was disrespectful, But overall, I had a really good childhood. Even after the regime changed. My mom and my stepdad are truly those who are responsible for my morals and ethics. Well, maybe a few of those ass beatings to make sure it sunk in. Needless to say, I never asked nor mentioned anything about Amou Reza's job then nor any time after my journey to the States. Especially after the fall of Shah's regime. If the new Islamic Government would have found out, he would have been tortured and executed. He was a beast of a man but a big old teddy bear inside. He was my idol and set a lot of good examples for me as I grew up.

My mother, who I see as the supermom, was a badass too. Standing at 4 feet 11 inches tall, she strutted around, very professional and direct in her all-white nurse's outfit and that funny nurse cap that resembles a navy soldier. Before I had started school, my mom used to take me to the hospital with her, and I would roam the hallways and just about do whatever I wanted. At six years old, accompanying her to work one day, I was running down one of the hallways when my mom walked into the hall from the second building. She didn't say a word. I didn't even see her, but I felt that smack on the back of my head as I made the corner right in front of her, running in the same direction as she was walking. She might be short, but man, she was quick. She demanded respect, and she got it. Not to mention, in our culture, the mother is the most respected member of the family. Even in Islam, the religion practiced by nearly two billion people worldwide, a mother is held to the highest standard.

Some religious texts from the seventh century mention Prophet Mohammad saying when asked by a man about his mother, that "Your Heaven lies under the feet of your mother." These are contributors as to why Middle Easterners are always taking the extra steps to ensure that their mother is always cared for, even in bad health. In some families, mothers who are no longer able to take care of themselves or suffer illnesses that hinder their ability to perform daily activities are taken into their household and cared for until their time is called. Sadly, for most of the Western culture, when an elderly parent is no longer able to care for themselves, they are admitted to an elderly care facility rather than being taken in by one of the children.

Si O Se Pol, the largest ancient bridge that spans across the Zayanderud River, is comprised of thirty-three poles. It is a dam and a bridge that was built in the 1590s by the King of the Safavid Empire. It was built to connect the elite of the time, who lived on one side of the river, to the largely Armenian neighborhoods on the opposite side of the river. Armenians, who are Christian, were and still are one of the largest religious groups who live in Iran. Prior to the fall of the Shah of Iran in 1979, Jews were also an integral part of the Iranian population. Most Jews fled Iran for Europe, Israel, and the United States after the revolution in fear of losing all their assets. They transferred most of what they could and restarted their lives outside of Iran.

My stepdad, cousins, and close relatives used to frequent Si O Se Pol on Thursday nights, where some would fish, and some would have a picnic and play music on the steps of the dam. Most smoked Ghalyoun (hookah) at these gatherings. It was a national park where outdoor picnics were common. I remember attending many birthday parties at Si O Se Pol. But, just like any other metropolitan city, the area also attracted the homeless and addicts. I remember playing around and running between the openings in the structure, and in some corners of the bridge, we would see aluminum foil and hypodermic needles used by drug addicts. At a young age, we were taught a lot of street smarts. We knew what drugs were, and just like in any other country, drug addicts will throw their refuse near hidden areas in public venues.

At one of these gatherings, I accompanied my next-door neighbor and their kids, and as we played football at the banks of the river, one of the kids kicked the ball right into the water. The river was high that day, and the authorities had opened several of the dam walls of the bridge to allow the water to flow. This caused the river to flow faster, creating an undertow current near the banks of the river. One of the kids, around ten years old, ran into the water after the ball. The water level where he entered was about a meter high, but the current was pulling the ball away from the shore, and it was starting to gain momentum downstream. The kid, who I didn't know, lunged towards the ball and, within a split second, disappeared from view. Looked like he had just sunk. Not even five seconds later, his head popped up in the middle of the river, and we could hear his screams. Everyone around the bank started screaming, and just about everyone started to run down the side of the bank looking for a good place to enter the water. One guy dove into the river, fully clothed, and started to swim to the mainstream. He was fast. Really fast! He was going at an angle toward the boy, who was rapidly being taken further down the stream. We were all running down the side of the river, in the same direction as the current, as a few other guys jumped in the water to attempt to get ahead of the boy's location.

The longer we ran, which seemed to have been about 900 meters by now, the faster the boy would go. This is all happening within a minute of when the boy first entered the water. Suddenly, the boy disappeared. We couldn't see any part of his body in the raging water, and the last location we saw him was about 100 meters from the shore. No one knew what to do. His mother was screaming and crying for help, asking every man in sight to please rescue her son.

A few seconds later, a boat appeared coming up the stream, and I assume they had figured out someone was in the water. It turned out to be a police patrol boat. Using a bullhorn, one of the policemen on the boat asked if someone had been lost in the water. Everyone started to scream and shout, pointing to the last location where the boy was seen. In an instant, the boat made a 180-degree turn and started to speed up downstream. Right before the boat was about to go around a bend in the river, one of the policemen on the boat dove into the water, and another policeman pitched out a rope into the water. The next thing we see is the water splash, and the policeman surfaces, holding the lifeless body of the boy. He grabbed the rope, and the boat crew pulled him and the boy into the boat. We couldn't see what they were doing because the interior of the boat was deep, and the distance from shore was far enough that no one could make out what was happening.

I am standing near the bank of the river, on a large rock, along with what I would guess were about fifty other individuals, listening to the chatter. What stood out was the whaling of the boy's mother. She was screaming at the top of her lungs, saying, "Ya Khoda, Ya Ali, Bache ma ra beyar." Translating that, she was saying, "Great God, Great Ali, bring my baby back." "Ali" is the name of the Grandson of Prophet Mohammad, who was raised at a young age by the Prophet and ultimately became the Prophet's Son-In-Law by his marriage to Fatimah, the Prophet's daughter. These two figures are the center of the Shia Sect of Islam. They are referred to as the AhlulBayt (The Holy Household). I'll talk more about this later in the book, as it is a significant part of the sectarian issues between the two branches of Islam.

What does "Ya Ali" mean? For Shia Muslims, Ali was the cousin and son-in-law of the Islamic prophet Muhammad and a member of the Ahl al-Bayt. According to Shias, Ali was the first Imam who is believed to be the rightful and divine successor to Muhammad. Ahl al-Bayt ("People of the House") refers to the holy family of the Islamic prophet Muhammad, particularly his daughter Fatimah, her husband Ali (who was also Muhammad's cousin), and their sons al-Husayn and Hasan. The term has also been extended in Sunni Islam to apply to all descendants of the Banu Hashim and even to all Muslims.

As the commotion was raging and the screams of the mother were overpowering everyone else's voices, I saw a policeman stand up in the boat, where his upper torso was clearly visible, he threw his arms in the air with the index finger and middle finger making the form of a V. This is the symbol for victory in Farsi. The same concept as throwing the "Thumbs Up" in the West, meaning "All Is Good." This meant, universally, to everyone on the banks that the boy was okay. The sound of the loud sighs filled the air. It was a moment of relief, and the feeling that overcame everyone was one of joy. I looked around, even with tears in my own eyes, watching so many people who didn't know each other cry with joy. The mother, who was still crying, but now because of happiness, started to grab every person around her and kiss them on the cheeks, raising her hands to the sky and saying "Alhamdulillah," meaning "Praise God." She was so excited, yet anxious at the bank of the river as the boat made its way to where we were standing.

The boat came about thirty meters from the bank, and two of

the four policemen holding the boy came off the boat and walked the boy ashore. I walked my way between the bystanders, and as the two policemen stepped up on the rocks into the grassy area, I looked at the boy. He was awake but seemed very disoriented. He was crying and looked scared. His mother, without missing a beat, grabbed the boy, kissed him, and handed him over to a male relative and immediately dropped to her knees and began kissing the feet of the policemen. A sign of an extreme level of gratitude, I was even crying nonstop. Even at a young age, I was experiencing such a show of love and affection by everyone who displayed genuine concern and the gratitude of a mother towards men she didn't know. An ambulance showed up a short time later, loaded the boy, his mother, and father, and off they went. To this day, every time I see images of Si O Se Pol, I relive those emotional moments I felt over forty years ago.

Persians are, by nature, very caring people. It is our culture to always spring up and lend a helping hand. If I was to write a book about the cultural traits of just Persians, it would come in volumes. It is a very rich culture, and for every scenario, there are certain etiquettes in place. Even as a Persian, some of the cultural traits become cumbersome for me. It comes with a certain level of drama if that makes sense. In a culture where there are expectations to react to certain situations in a certain way, you can imagine how it could be so stressful. Always having to be aware of everything and everyone around you and not being too rude or careless, to the point that at times, depending on the level of expectation, one can't focus on realistic goals. I guess I'm too Westernized because of the fact that I live a very busy life, I have to limit my interaction and involvement with a lot of Persians, or I would never get anything accomplished myself.

In Western culture, a family outing is promoted and somewhat expected. But, if a family member is traveling for work or is on the job and can't make the outing, it's completely under-standable. Oh no, not in Middle Eastern culture. In our culture, especially if you're living overseas, your family comes first. The job is second, and if there is a party for someone's birthday, wedding, or whatever, you're expected to come. No matter if you must take off work and lose a day's pay, you better be there. Or you'll never hear the end of it. It gets so dramatic at times that if you miss an event, every single family member, both close and distant, will continuously make derogatory comments in your presence. Some carry it on for years. Just imagine how many times you'd have to hear about not showing up to your third cousin's birthday party that you missed four years ago. And how many people in your extended family would make comments about it years later? That's so dramatic, even for me, and I'm fully aware of the culture.

Cultural traits and traditions should really be written and examined in volumes. They are so varied and require much explanation, especially when learning expectations and protocol. Manners and overall decorum are so deeply ingrained, much like British or French customs; the people hold steadfast to their traditions as part of their cultural identity. In every society, the family is the core. Relationships between men and women, how children are parented and raised, and how people provide for their families dictate much of how a culture thrives. In Iran, the quality of the family is vital, and its ability to thrive impacts society for generations. When you want to learn a country's culture, background, motivations, and mindset, look at the families.

Chapter 4
Molotov Cocktail

A Friday in the Middle East is like a one-day weekend. It's the day equivalent to the Sabbath in Judaism. It is a day of prayers and service to God, and just about every store is closed for business. It was determined in early Islam that Friday (Jummah) would be a day when Muslims could unite and have congregational prayers but not share the same days with the Jews or Christians out of respect for their day. On Jummah, Muslims are to go to their Masjid (Mosque) and partake in uniform prayers with other Muslims as the Ummah (One Body.) The term Ummah can be "Body" or "Nation," referring to a unified congregation. Therefore, one would hear the words "Ummah" being mentioned a lot when someone speaks of the "Religious Body/People."

On a Friday in the late 1970s, just a few months after the incident at Si O Se Pol, my mom, stepdad, and grandpa were in the living area, sitting on the floor, leaning against the pillows, watching television. As we watched, I heard my grandpa start to curse and mention that we are all about to be locked down. Of course, as a seven-year-old boy, I had no clue what my grandpa was talking about. But from his tone, I could tell he was pissed.

The Patriot Jihadi

I saw images and videos on our television showing protests and smoke coming off the sidewalks in what my grandpa said was Tehran. I remember having been to Tehran a few times to visit my dad's family, but still wasn't able to figure out what was going on. All I knew was that he was pissed and kept mentioning that the Shah was about to be killed.

My mom and stepdad sat there quietly, just staring at the television. I heard my stepdad whisper something to my mom, and I could only make out "bayad pesareto befresim Amerika," which translates to "We have to send your son to America." I didn't know what was happening, but I knew from my mom's worried facial expressions something bad was about to happen. I walked over from where I was playing with my dump truck and my army tank on the floor next to the couch and asked my mom, "Chera man bayad beram Amrika?" (Why do I have to go to America?)

The problem in my mind was that my father lived in the States, and I had not seen or spoken to him. I had no clue who he was. He didn't have much to do with me. I guess he blamed my mom for choosing to take care of her father and leaving him, so he pretty much cut ties with us. If you're reading this and thinking like the Western culture that he should have been ordered to support, child support is just that; a practice in Western culture. The laws are totally different overseas.

Traditionally, no matter the religious practices, tribal culture handles certain things in a specific way. For example, if a marriage ends in divorce, no matter the religion, the children stay with the mother until the boy is seven and the girl is nine. That is the time of nurturing and when the mother's presence has the most impact in the child's life. Once the children get to the ages mentioned, the custody is automatically changed to the father. This is the norm for the more traditional countries. At the same time, in some countries that are ruled by Islamic Law, this process is also implemented as law based on "Islamic

Canonical" law that we all have heard about. It's referred to as Sharia Law and the most common term we hear about in the West. Since my dad was in America and my mom was in Iran, he couldn't get me under Iranian laws, and I don't think he would have anyway.

My mom answered, "Een dolat avaz mishe va nemidoonim shekar mikonan be bache-ha" (The government is about to change, and we don't know what will happen to everyone's kids.) This statement made no sense to me. It wasn't until a few years later that I realized what they had been fearful about. I will share more about these experiences when I write about the school-age events later on in the book.

From that day, it almost became a daily ritual that we watched the news. We saw the conflicts in Tehran grow more and more over the following weeks. The university students clashed with the Shah's army and policemen daily. A few weeks later, the protests erupted in Esfahan, and young teenagers and college students started to march in the streets and throw Molotov cocktails at the police and the army. At that age, most things didn't make sense, but I could tell in my gut that something bad was about to happen. Now that I think back, as a child, I was also afraid of the uncertainty that would follow. I could clearly see the fear in my mom, stepdad, and grandpa's eyes. They tried to minimize whatever was going on since I didn't understand, but their demeanor and quiet talks sure did make things a bit suspicious. At the same time, all I cared about were my toys and if I would get to go out and play football with my friends in the street. At times, I was on the Army's side because I had grown up playing with Army soldier figures, and their uniforms appealed to me.

I spent a lot of time outside my home. We had a bunch of kids in the neighborhood, and between playing football as we acted like we were the Iranian National Football Team and climbing the rooftops of the houses to sneak into the orchard near the neighborhood to steal pomegranates and figs, there really wasn't anything else to do. So, the protests and the fear that was looming around sure made that part even scarier. Sometimes, listening to my mom and stepdad talk, I expected the homes to be locked down and no one to be able to leave. Can you imagine a boy being locked down? Especially a boy like me who was 100 miles per hour from the time my feet hit the ground until I passed out at night. I'm still like that. I hit the ground running in the morning and never stop until I lay on my bed. After thirty seconds, I'm snoring as if I've been asleep for four hours. They say there are stages of sleep that one transitions to before that deep state. My sleep? Yeah, it's 100 MPH to deep sleep in thirty seconds, and when I open my eyes, it's dead rest to 100 MPH in thirty seconds. The only thing that slows me down now is the little aches and pains in my knees and my back when I bounce off my bed in the morning. I guess old age does have its effects on the body after a lifetime of abuse.

Every day, I would go out and play with my friends in the street, until one day, as we were kicking the football around and shooting into a makeshift goal, an SUV drove onto our street. It was creeping on us slowly. We recognized it. At least I did. I yelled at my friend "Artesh Oomadeh" (The Army is Here.) We all stopped. The SUV stopped about ten meters from us, and an Army soldier slowly got out of the passenger side. The man, who was like a jolly green giant, stepped into the street and straightened his shirt. He motioned for us to go to him. I was scared. We started to walk slowly as a group to him. There were five of us. The oldest was twelve, and I was the youngest at seven years old. I stayed behind the others since they were all taller than me. When we got to the front bumper of the SUV, the man walked over to us and kneeled down. He then transitioned to a squatting position and smiled. His voice became very soothing, and in a very low tone of voice and quietly, he told us that it was getting dangerous down the next street over and we need to go inside our homes. He said he didn't want the protestors to harm us if we happened to be in the streets should they come over.

It wasn't but ten seconds after he said that and stood back up, looking back at the driver, when all of a sudden, something hit the back of the SUV, and a fireball erupted. The fireball was from a "Molotov Cocktail." He ducked down, and at the same time, the driver opened the door and rolled over onto the ground to the left side of the SUV. I thought he was hurt. He started yelling for us to run. We all took off in the opposite direction, heading back to the alleyway that led to our homes. Piroozi Street is where we were playing. As I was running, I realized I had left my football near the makeshift goal, and when I turned around to see what was behind me, I saw about ten or fifteen teenagers, wearing a cloth over their faces to not inhale in smoke and tear gas, throwing rocks and other hard items at the Army SUV. I was in shock. I paused for a minute, almost out of breath. I saw one of them towards the back of the group kneel down, and as soon as he stood to his feet, I saw him throw a bottle with fire at the end of it at the SUV again. As soon as that bottle crashed on the street next to the SUV, there was an explosion, and another fireball started.

Half the street was in flames, and half of the SUV was on fire. I turned around and started running again, with my friends now being about forty meters ahead of me. We had a good way to run before we could turn left on the alleyway that took us to our homes. In the midst of running away, I heard footsteps behind me. I kicked it in a higher gear and turned my head to look over my shoulder. I saw the two soldiers running fast toward us and running away from the fireball. As my friends and I turned left on our alleyway, the two soldiers continued straight. I have no clue what happened to them after that because I didn't stick around to find out. I ran straight home, opened the big metal door to my grandpa's house, closed it, locked it, and ran straight for the kitchen.

I opened the glass door that went from our concrete courtyard into the kitchen. My mom, who was cooking dinner, looked at me and immediately asked, "Chieh Shaheen, chera tarsidi?" "What is it, Shaheen, what's scaring you?" She could definitely tell I was scared. I told her what had happened. She ran to the front door again to make sure it was locked. Then she came back and picked up the home phone to call my stepdad's work. She got a hold of him and told him about what I had said. I could hear him get upset and hear him say to her not to go out and stay inside. The one thing that made us less worried was that when watching the news and hearing about protests, we hadn't heard of any mobs attacking the normal population. Their beef was with the Shah's police and army. But that still didn't make things pleasant.

This kind of event went on for a few weeks, and of course, being Persians and because the culture causes everyone to talk about things all the time, we started hearing that a guy named Ayatollah Khomeini was in France and was working with the young university students to overthrow the Shah of Iran. I didn't understand all this, but it was the main topic of conversation between everyone and even on some television channels. I remember hearing that some students had taken over the United States Embassy in Tehran, holding all the Americans Hostage. I had no clue what an embassy was and had no clue that there were Americans in Iran. I remember asking my mom why there were Americans in Iran and if I was an American, are they going to kidnap me too.

She tried simplifying it and told me that the Americans in Iran were in Tehran, and there were a lot of Americans in Iran because the Shah was good friends with the Americans. She told me that even though I was Iranian because I was born in America, I was too an American citizen. She did comfort me by saying they're kidnapping the Americans who are not of Iranian origin. I had no clue what that meant, but from the images I had seen on TV, I didn't look like an American. Most Americans on TV had blonde hair and blue eyes, but not me. I had thick wavy black hair and dark brown eyes, olive skin, and sure didn't speak the language. But hey, if Mom says I'm American, then so be it. That's how things go in the Middle East. When your parents tell you something is a certain way, it's pretty much the gospel. Even if they're wrong and you know to the contrary, you don't ever argue your point unless you want to be slapped across the face, a cooking spoon thrown at you, or just a swift smack to the back of your head. It's the culture, and elders are always right; always! You simply listen and agree–end of story!

A few weeks later, while I was in the living room watching TV, the channel stopped, and all I could see was the fuzzy screen. A few minutes later, a constant multicolored screen resembling a rainbow appeared, and a very high-pitched tone sounded, the ones that show that the broadcast is over. But it was the middle of the afternoon, and that tone and image usually came on the TV after midnight, when the TV stations would close. I ran into my mom's room and could hear her speaking to my Khaleh (Aunt). She has two sisters and a brother. The uncle from the mother's side in Farsi is called "Daii." Both my aunts lived in Iran, and my Daii had moved to the States back in the late 60s as well to pursue a career in accounting and the legal field.

Listening to my mom on the phone with my Khaleh Zari (that's Aunt Zari). I realized it was about the protests. Obviously, I'm nosey, so I sneak closer and act like I'm looking for something under the bed. I hear my Khaleh Zari tell my mom that her two sons have been out there protesting and throwing rocks at the "Artesh" (Army). By this point, my nosiness has now got me in a competitive mode. How could my cousins do fun stuff but I can't? Of course, I did not understand the whole protest thing or politics. All I knew at that point was that my cousins were out with the crowd and having "fun," while I was cooped up in a house and couldn't leave because of the fear of being hurt by the protestors.

Now, about the whole nosey thing. I'm not a sneaky person, but nosey is pretty much embedded in all Middle Easterners. We all know that family drama is everyone's business in the extended family, and if someone screws up one thing or succeeds at another, the entire family is somehow involving themselves and talking about it. That's how folks are here stateside too. But, with Persians, imagine that concept but on 1000 MG of Testosterone and it's the center of the culture. If a Persian anywhere in the world does something negative or positive, his/her family, neighborhood, and if in a small village, the entire population is aware, talking about, and giving their opinions about it. Much like living in a small town in the South, places like Mississippi in towns of 1000 or less. That type of drama and nosiness, but much worse. I mean, it's so dramatic that if you want to get married, the entire village feels they have a say so and should give guidance.

Once I knew my cousins were out and not getting hurt, I got

this smart idea that I would also sneak out and go to the protests. You would think my mom would have a coronary and would be very strict. But, my mom was laid back when it came to letting me explore. I knew that the worst thing that could happen is I'd get a good ass whooping or an ear twisting with a few slaps behind the head, as I would be escorted from the front door to our living room when I got home. It was a risk, but I am a risk taker to some extent once I can relate to someone involved in that same risk. So, knowing my cousins were okay and had been doing it for a few weeks, I drummed up the balls to try it.

One afternoon, after "Namaz-e Zohr" (Mid-Day Prayers), I told my mom that I was going to Payam's house. Payam was one of the kids I played with in the street, who lived about five houses down the alleyway from us. My mom told me to come back before dark, so we could do our Namaz'e Maghreb (Evening Prayers). I left home and snuck into the main street about one kilometer from my house. It's the same street that led to "Tohid Square." As I rounded the corner, I saw a large group of college students holding up signs with a picture of the Shah and some blonde-haired dude. Both were covered by a huge X. There was an older man who owned the shoe store at the corner who was outside of his store smoking a cigarette. I asked the man what the guys were doing. He responded, "Mikhan Shah-o Biroonesh Konan" (They want to kick the Shah out of Iran). Being nosey and still having no clue who the blonde-haired guy was, I asked the man, "Oon Aks-e Ki-e?" (Who's in the other picture?) He said, "Rayees-e Jomhouri-e Amerikast. Esmesh Jimmy Carter-e" (He's the President of America. His name is Jimmy Carter). I had no clue what that meant, but I did have a bit of a kind favor for the man since he was American, and so was I. I kind of felt betrayed that my people were hating on my other people.

I started to walk to the square, and as I passed a Kabobi

Restaurant, I saw about thirty other college-aged guys come out, all holding the same kind of signs, walking up behind me as we were headed towards the other group of about 500 or more guys protesting. As I got closer, I could hear them chant, but couldn't make it out. It wasn't until I heard the crowd behind me start repeating the same chant. It was clear as day. They were chanting "Marg Bar Amrika" (Death to America). I paused for a minute and was confused. I was trying to understand why the American people were being hated on and wished death upon when the only Americans I had seen were the ones I saw on TV at the Embassy. I asked one of the guys, "Chera Migeen Marg bar Amerika?" (Why are you wishing death on Americans?) They all stopped. I got a little scared until one guy with a Shemagh (Arabic Headscarf for men) around his neck looked at me, smiled, and went on to say it was because the Shah was in power because of America, and he was helping Americans take our oil, while the Shah was keeping all the money. That made sense, even to me as a young boy. Not that I knew anything about how that stuff worked, but I'm Persian, and that meant that something that belonged to us was being given to someone else, and one person was benefiting from it alone instead of the whole population.

It kind of made me angry that the Shah was being selfish. But at that age, all I knew was that everyone was against the Shah, and I was right there in the middle of them. As all this was going on, I began to think about me being an American, and if these folks hate Americans so much, what if they find out? I'd be the perfect person to get hurt by them. So, I decided to just run along with them to the protest jhnd start chanting the same things so I wouldn't seem out of place. It was kind of cool at the same time. Here I am at seven years old, hanging around a bunch of men and feeling like I was part of something. Heck, I hadn't been outside for weeks and had all this energy built up. So, it was exciting to say the least. Besides, I felt like an adult.

As I chanted and started to make my right hand into a fist and raised it above my head with every syllable, I felt more comfortable and welcomed. I found myself in the middle of the large crowd, which had grown to over two thousand by that point, and the chanting was so loud I couldn't hear anything else. No nature, no cars, no honking of the car horns. Nothing but chanting. Suddenly, a guy to my right, who had been chanting loudly, picked me up and put me on his shoulders. I had no clue who the guy was. All I knew was he picked me up, put me on his shoulders, and handed me the sign he had in his hands. One of the signs that had Jimmy Carter on it. So, what do I do? Of course, I had to participate. If I didn't, I had no clue what would have happened.

We repeated the chant for about fifteen minutes until we heard a bullhorn squelch. We all stopped. It was the police and the army. One guy from the army started telling us that we need to leave or we'll be getting hit with tear gas. All the while I was thinking, "Wait a minute! These are the soldiers who came to our street and told us to leave so we don't get hurt, but now they're going to shoot tear gas into the crowd?" I felt like I was caught between a rock and a hard place. The army soldiers helped us kids before, and now I'm in the middle of a crowd who seems to be friendly towards me. I was thinking about what I should do while on the shoulder of this guy I don't even know, holding his sign. I could tell it was about to get ugly, and I had this feeling that my mom was looking for me. I'm about fifteen minutes from my house and thought if she goes to Payam's house and I'm not there, I'm surely getting an ass whooping that will be over the top for lying to her.

As all this was going through my head, and as soon as the soldier lowered his bullhorn, I saw a Shah protest sign being thrown at the soldiers. And boy, that was it. The next thing I knew the crowd started throwing all kinds of stuff at the line of soldiers and cops that had now flanked the crowd. I yelled at the guy who was holding me up and told him to let me down, and he did. I handed him his sign and ran through the crowd back toward Piroozi Street. My heartbeat must have been over 200 because I could feel my heart about to pop out of my chest. My lungs were burning as I was at a full sprint down Tohid Boulevard, about to near the cut-off for Piroozi Street. I made the corner and heard shots and I slid to a stop, ducked down, and could see people running down the street behind me, away from the square. I moved over toward the side of the street and peeped around the corner. I could see smoke everywhere. It was blowing towards where I was and it wasn't but a second or two later when I felt burning in my nose and throat. I turned around and went back into a full sprint as I heard more gunshots, and they sounded like they were getting bigger and closer. If I was running an Olympic race that day, I would have won a gold medal for the fastest time in any of the races.

Midway down Piroozi Street, I had to stop because I couldn't breathe. My lungs were on fire, and snot was all over my face.

My eyes were watering, and I could hardly see. I gained my composure and made the last corner to the alleyway that led to my house. Then it dawned on me; "What am I going to tell my mom? I must go home, but she's thinking I was at Payam's house." When I turned the last corner that would lead me to our front door, I saw my mom outside in the alleyway, standing there with Payam and his mom. I froze in place. She saw me and started to walk very fast towards me. I was about eighty meters away, but as she got closer, I could see her face was changing from being angry to being concerned. When she got about twenty meters away, she started to run toward me and asked, "Chi Shod Shaheen Joon?" (What Happen, my dear Shaheen?) That was a reply of concern. She thought I was crying. I told her I smelled the tear gas and I was okay. Well, that didn't go over well. She immediately changed into an angry Persian mom and started to yell at me about lying to her and that I could have been killed. Of course, just like any kid at that age, what came next was what I had dreaded.

She grabbed me by my right ear lobe and escorted me to the front door of the house, as she twisted the cartilage of my ear so hard I thought she was about to tear it off my head. That was so painful I started to confess, just hoping for a break and hoping she would spare my ear. All she was telling me on that long 100-meter walk was, "Khafeh Sho!" (Shut Up!) To this day, if anything gets around my ear lobes, I feel the pain like I did that day. I think it gave me some sort of PTSD. It sounds funny now, but the pain was something else.

As we entered the main doors of the house, she released my ear. I grabbed my ear and could feel the heat emitting from it. I kept feeling it and looking at my hands to make sure it had not ripped anywhere. I guess the cartilage is really that strong. There were a couple of times in that walk when she almost picked me up by the ear; I'm surprised it didn't come off. As I was feeling my ear, she walked behind me into the living room and told my grandpa I had been off the street and on the main street. My Grandpa just looked at me, looked at her, and burst into laughter. His response surprised me a bit because I didn't expect that response, and neither did she. My Grandpa then continued by saying that boys will always be nosey, and it's by getting hurt doing stupid stuff is how they learn. I don't think my mom liked that response. She seemed pissed, but she didn't say a word. I know she was being respectful to her father, but I kind of felt like Grandpa was on my side. Boy, was I wrong! When my mom left the room, the Grandpa I envisioned came out. First, his face changed. Those thick bushy eyebrows formed a V, and his tone got lower and deeper as he told me to sit.

He had started to prepare the things he needed to smoke opium. As he was working on the charcoal and cutting the paste to place on his porcelain pipe, he looked up at me with a serious gaze. He said "Shoma Chera Rafteen To-e Khiaboon-e Bozorg?" (Why did you go to the main road?) I didn't know what to say. I was still holding my ear as the pain had not subsided yet, and the stinging was even worse. I told him I was curious and wanted to see. He realized I was just exploring and asked me to explain to him what had happened. I did, and the whole time, while explaining the event in detail, I was thinking at any moment he was going to get up and smack me in the face. He didn't say a word. Halfway through my recounting of the events, he raised his pipe and took a big hit off the Taryak. He then blew out the smoke and took a second one. He held it in and motioned for me to come to him. I thought he was about to slap me. He grabbed my ear and blew the smoke to the side of my head and into my ear. The pain was gone in an instant.

I asked him if he was mad, and he didn't answer. He just sat there looking at me, dead in my eyes, so I dropped my head and started to tear up. I was ashamed of disrespecting my mom and my grandpa. He knew I was! He put his hand on my shoulder as I sat next to him and said to me, "Shoma Bayad Be Madaretoon

Goosh Bedeen" (You must listen to your mom.) I already knew this, but he was reinforcing the whole respect thing we must show for parents and elders. He then continued to say that The Prophet has said that those who disrespect their parents are viewed as sinners in the eyes of Allah (God). In our culture, this sentiment is echoed repeatedly in all stages of life. It becomes the foundation of family unity and respect. It is passed down from parent to child for generations. This concept is also a main contributor to how some children are brainwashed by parents who have ill will. If a parent has extremist views, the demand and conditioning of respect for parents and elders contribute to a child being indoctrinated. At least I knew that my grandpa didn't have ill will. He was teaching me morals about how to be a good and respectable human. There was no way I would ever be conditioned or indoctrinated to be hateful or an extremist because I had balance at a young age when it came to Islamic principles. My grandpa wasn't a scholar, but he was a good man and he was very knowledgeable. I later found myself in situations where I was being exposed to extremist ideologies. Even though I had to participate as a student in school, my solid foundation and education from my grandpa and my mother enabled me to stay on the right path and not be influenced by the tactics used. I lived it, and through all the indoctrination attempts and participation in various activities, I still was able to identify what was right or wrong.

Chapter 5
The Master – Al-Sayyid

First grade in Iran wasn't like your typical first grade in the States. After the fall of the Shah and his exile to the West, Ayatollah Ruhollah Khomeini returned to Iran from France, where he took reign as the "Supreme Leader." In Farsi, he was referred to as "Rahbar." He wore a black turban, which is worn by those who are direct descendants of The Prophet Mohammad. Those whose lineage goes back to Ali Ibn Abu Talib and Fatimah Bint Mohammad, the daughter of The Prophet. I too am a Seyed, and if I was to become an Imam, I would wear the black turban.

The fact that I was a Seyed was an essential part of why I had to have guidance in Islamic Theology. As a Seyed, the culture requires you to be most knowledgeable on the topic of religion since most of the population always asks a Seyed for guidance and religious interpretations. In the Middle Eastern culture, being from a certain lineage comes with a lot of requirements. If a member coming from a certain lineage is unfamiliar with their history, they are viewed as incompetent. The pride that is ingrained by culture is the driving force behind one's pursuit of excellence on the topic they are required to know inside out. My title as a Seyed required me to know details that most Muslims would not be required to study. This was the motivating factor behind my grandpa and mom's attempt to educate me through various channels.

Who is Ayatollah Khomeini? His full name was Ruhollah Mostafavi Musavi, an Iranian political and religious leader from 1979 until his death in 1989. He was the founder of the Islamic Republic of Iran and the leader of the 1979 Iranian Revolution, which saw the overthrow of Shah Mohammad Reza Pahlavi and the end of the Persian monarchy. Following the revolution, Khomeini became the country's first supreme leader, a position created in the constitution of the Islamic Republic as the highest-ranking political and religious authority of the nation, which he held until his death. He was succeeded by Ali Khamenei in June 1989. After Ali Khamenei, the following became President in order: Akbar Hashemi, Rafsanjani, Mohammad Khatami, Mahmoud Ahmadinejad, Hassan Rouhani, and Ebrahim Raisi.

I remember screwing up at school one day and the principal called my mom. I vividly recall him reminding my mom that as a Seyed, I was being held to a higher standard, and even though other kids could get away with certain things, I was expected to walk that fine line. Imagine the level of expectation that would be attached to everything you do if you're a preacher's son. Now, multiply that concept by a thousand and imagine if a person was to have been the direct descendant of Moses or even Jesus Christ. He would be viewed in a way where most would expect the person to have vast knowledge about his lineage all the way back to Moses or Jesus' time on earth. Failing to possess the knowledge would be devastating to the entire family's reputation. It would appear that the family was not prideful nor respected their lineage. YES! That is how things are viewed in the deep-rooted Middle Eastern culture. One is expected to master the craft of their lineage when it comes to theological, historical, and tribal background.

What is a Seyyed? - Persian: 'Lord' or 'Master'; a masculine name given to descendants of the Islamic prophet Muhammad (and his grandson Hussein); a Muslim honorary title. – Arabic: 'a noble one'. The title is usually used in front of the given name, or is used as a surname in honor of their ancestor.

At an early age, I learned what it meant to be a Seyed. As a little boy, my heroes were not only soldiers in uniform or men in capes, they were also the noble men and women who were the descendants of the prophet Muhammad. I share this noble ancestry, as does my son. When I was his age, I was taught that I was held to a higher standard in religious circles as well as in cultural customs, especially holidays and social practices. I began to learn customs and traditions that not all Iranians knew or practiced. (Many Iranians at that time, and still today, consider themselves Muslim by name only, more as a cultural affiliation. At that time, there were also many Iranians who were Jewish, Baha'i, Christian, Zoroastrian, or believed in other faiths.) I began to have a deeper sense of pride in these practices, feeling like part of a privileged class that not all my peers could understand. I attended special classes and events that aligned with those that shared the same ancestral lineage. To clarify, this was not related to the government-run religious programming. This early education was directly related to me being a Seyed and could be easily compared to parents choosing to put their children in a vacation Bible school or Catechism class that has deeper emphasis on a specific faith.

This was different from the government-mandated religious teachings based on Sharia law that I would experience in my regular school days. During and after the Iranian Revolution, government officials were placed in posts in schools to teach Islamic studies and general subjects. Many had no educational background or experience with child development. They were simply there to do a job, which was to promote a religious and cultural agenda through propaganda, memorized rhetoric, and visual images to children from the approximate age of six years old until graduation from high school. The new style of education included religious elements in all subjects. Idolizing religious and political figures became a standardized practice in schools. Deliberate and focused education for the youth of the country from a young age has been a practice in many countries around the world, and for good reason. When you teach a child from a young age, they will become loyal to not only the education but also the educators themselves. Even when parents or extended family may have disagreed with the change in school education, the children had no choice but to conform, obey and adapt to their daily school environment, day after day, year after year.

Sharia Law – Islam's legal system, derived from the Qur'an, Islam's holy book, as well as the Sunnah and Hadith; the deeds and sayings of the Prophet Muhammad. Where an answer cannot be derived directly from these, religious scholars may give rulings based on their interpretation, as guidance on a particular topic or question. Most Muslim-majority countries incorporate Sharia at some level in their legal framework, not unlike countries that use Judeo-Christian values to establish their legal system. Example: Iran and Saudi Arabia have Islamic law-based regulations that require women to wear a veil over their hair (and in some cases their face/body) and to

The Patriot Jihadi

The ideologies taught from a young age affect how they view other people and cultures around the world. When we hear of terrorist activities and the background of certain individuals, we often learn of religious *madrassahs* (schools) as the earliest form of indoctrination. The religious indoctrination becomes the overpowering component, more so than the value of human life or learning other moral elements that we might consider essential in forming a young mind. For many who read this, you may now recognize the parallel in recent events with schools implementing new ideologies regarding gender identities and how certain social agendas are being pushed by teachers from elementary schools all the way to universities. There is always a connection between the administration that places key individuals in certain positions, and it's never an accident. The individual's background, connections, and motivations influence what they teach and how they teach, and the youth are always the ones that pay the highest price.

From the first grade, I can remember the beginning of this new education in school. My days started early, but we had a long lunch break in the middle of the day, where kids would typically go home for lunch with their families and afternoon prayers "*zuhr*" or "*duhr.*" Then we would return to school for the afternoon session until 5 o'clock in the evening. Fridays were our religious days off, so we had long days and long weeks. When American children struggle through full-day kindergarten, I think back to what we endured as children in Iran. There was no negotiating your child's schedule or making accommodations for a child that couldn't sit still long enough without a nap or a recess.

We had pictures of religious and political figures in our class-rooms. We were shown videos and photos of various Islamic groups, like Hezbollah, that shared beliefs and practices with the Islamic Regime of Iran. We learned how to recognize different countries and cultural elements within the various groups. At my elementary school, we began having mandatory military training three times a week instead of recess. A similar practice was implemented during World War II in Hitler's Germany, with young children being taught songs and slogans to align with the Third Reich. The children were forced to exchange religious classes and free play for a more regimented program, but the goal was the same. When children are taught to think beyond their own natural, self-centered perspective, they begin to have a loyalty to their entire class or community and even country. The individual loses value unless it becomes part of a bigger goal. As a child, I began to idolize the military figures in town and embraced the opportunity to begin wearing a uniform during our school training. Children always want to be part of something bigger and more important, so it was natural for me to want to emulate the men I'd see in school or around the city where I lived.

The military training started off simply by familiarizing us with different weapons and tools used daily or in combat. They showed us photos of members of Hezbollah with their weapons, indicating a connection between their martyrdom and the weapons they used to complete their missions. We began to have a high regard for those who sacrificed their lives for Allah and for the greater Muslim community. They created a sense of anticipation so we would look forward to learning more and having the opportunity to hold the weapons ourselves and begin practicing with our own hands. We would then come back to the classrooms for the theory portion of the training. We would learn the religious laws, the diagrams of weapons and how they worked, practice samples that we were able to touch and become familiar with, and scenarios for how we might interact in the future. We learned how to march in the courtyards, how to tie our shoes, and how to dress properly. We were learning to be soldiers of God, not just for our country. We also learned who our religious and political enemies were and developed a sense of connection with like-minded countries versus those who we were taught were against our religion and values.

Not only was I excited to be part of these lessons, but because I was a Seyed, I was expected to excel. I would come to have a balance because I would go home to my mother and *Amu Reza* and ask them questions about what I had learned in school. They would correct me and explain that there were certain things being taught that were not actually in the Quran or were being misinterpreted. It's important to remember that not all who were teaching in the schools after the Revolution were trained educators or even experts in the subjects they were teaching. They were posted government officials from the Islamic Regime, appointed by mullahs to teach and promote their agenda in the name of education and religion.

Eventually, they started busing us to a nearby military base where we would have hands-on training with live weapons. No one prepared me for the impact that the shooting of these weapons would have on me physically, but I quickly learned that shooting a weapon that was almost the same height as me would be no easy task. I have always embraced challenges, and at that time, I wanted nothing more than to be like the military men I had been admiring from afar for some time. But when I shot the weapon the first time, the kickback was so strong that when it knocked me in the ear, it reminded me of the pain I felt when my mom twisted the hell out of my ear.

It may be shocking for most people to imagine a young child in first or second grade learning how to shoot weapons, and not just a small pistol either; military-grade weapons combined with the expectations of shooting like grown men. But for a country like Iran, with a new government and no trained military that was loyal to the new regime, they had to begin training boys at a young age in order to prepare them for active duty by the age of fifteen. The men and women who were for the Revolution were predominantly university students and young people under the age of thirty. While some did perform in military and law enforcement posts, many were continuing their education after the Revolution, so it was necessary to build a loyal military from scratch. The Islamic Regime was not only in volatile conflict with its own citizens but also with neighboring Arab countries as well. Little did I know, while in the midst of school and military training as a little boy, life in Iran was about to change yet again.

Chapter 6
Kaboom

In 1980, Saddam Hussain in Iraq initiated war against Iran. The Iraqis believed that because of the weak state of Iran's social climate, they would take cues from the Iranian people and revolt against their government. There has been animosity between Persians and Arabs for centuries, and while culturally, they share many similarities, it is deeply rooted in history. In terms of religious differences, the Shiite and Sunni Muslims have also had conflict and animosity, mostly stemming from doctrinal differences.

When my mother got mad at me for marrying a Palestinian Arab, it was because Palestinians are usually Sunni Muslims. In my former wife's case, she was actually Christian, which decreased my mother's anxiety over our theological differences. You rarely see a Sunni and Shiite marriage because of this sectarian conflict. Shiites believe that the reigns went down from Mohammad to his family and descendants. Sunnis believe that the followers and companions of Mohammad were the successors of Mohammad. This split has caused a sectarian divide and conflict ever since the prophet's death and will continue until they come to the table to reach a compromise.

Shawn Pardazi

Ever heard of peace in the Middle East? Yeah, me neither! Don't hold your breath!

The Iran-Iraq War from 1980 to 1988 began with the Iraqi invasion of Iran, with the rationale being the need to prevent the exporting of new ideologies to Iraq and the potential exploitation of sectarian tensions in Iraq between their Shia citizens against their officially secular and Sunni-dominated Iraqi government. Iraq also wished to replace Iran as the new power player within the region in the absence of Shah Pahlavi of Iran after the Islamic Revolution.

Shiites are the followers of the "holy household," or the *Ahlul beyt*. Sunnis follow the *Sunna of Mohammad*, which means "lifestyle and practices." It's an extremely complex topic to dive into, and I'm not a scholar of religion or history, so if you're interested in learning about the differences, refer to the book written by Author Lesley Hazelton called "After the Prophet." She spent years researching this topic and dives deep into the roots of the split between Shia and Sunni sects after Prophet Mohammad died.

When I was in school, we would take the passenger bus to military training in the afternoons. I was still young, but I had been issued an AK-47 with a bayonet that was practically my height! I had fallen over and almost stabbed myself in the face a few times in the past. One time I jumped into a hole and sliced my shirt open with the bayonet. As a child, I idolized the soldiers I witnessed. But, we couldn't disagree or even express disappointment without fear of government officials taking matters into their own hands. This was the start of the Iran-Iraq war that took many lives, left families estranged, and was a prominent time in the Middle East.

Hatred toward the West continued to intensify. In Iran, I was growing into a pre-teen, and military training became a bigger part of my education. They were speeding up training in preparation for the boys to be sent off to war at the age of fifteen. The war with Iraq continued to wreak havoc on many parts of Iran, especially the southwest border towns like Abadan. We had land mine detection training, where we were taught to continually stab the dirt with a knife in order to detect the land mines.

During a three-week session of learning about mines and how to find them, while crawling the ground at the military training facility, I vividly remember stabbing into the sand to find out if the tip of the knife I was given would hit metal. It was a slow and methodical process we had to master. But then imagine, here I am, a kid who wants to zip through the process to finish first. All males are born with a sense of competitiveness, and Middle Eastern men are no different. The pride of finishing off first and beating everyone else is in the back of every man's mind. So, there I was, stabbing away at an angle to see if I could find a mine while watching the next kid about one meter to my right. With my left hand feeling the top layer of the sand, I stabbed right through the soft tissue of my hand. Now, the mines we were detecting were inert or dummy mines. So, as I stabbed myself, I jumped up and threw the knife on the ground, grabbed my left hand, and blood began rushing through the six-centimeter cut, mixed with sand and dirt, and it had an intense burning sensation. As I stood up, a soldier ran to me from behind and smacked me in the back of the head, and yelled at me to lay back down. He then began pointing his finger at me and said if I did that on the battlefield, I'd be shot dead and rendered useless to the cause. There I was, in pain and wanting to get this blood to stop, but all they seemed to care about is how I stopped the process. Even at a young age, and even though I was mesmerized by the fact that I was training to be a soldier of God, I couldn't help but sense that my life was not important.

I would hear from friends and relatives with sons who died just shortly after going off to war – young boys of fifteen who barely had a chance of survival. Kids were getting blown up, and they would just send the bodies back to the families and move in another set of kids on the front lines. Mothers would warn others about the chance of losing children to the war. My mother's fear and concern over her only child increased, and I began to overhear conversations between her and my stepfather about what could be done to avoid me going into mandatory service.

My friend, Payam, was older than me, and at fifteen, he was sent off to war. I remember his mother coming to my house, sobbing and trying to explain what happened to him. The IRGC's Sepah had come to collect all the fifteen-year-old boys from the school without any opportunity for parents and family to say their goodbyes. Can you imagine sending your child to school and then being told your child has been sent off to war, most likely never to be seen alive again? That horrific roller coaster of emotions was what my friend's mother was experiencing when she showed up at our house.

The Patriot Jihadi

IRGC is the Islamic Revolutionary Guard Corps or "Army of the Guardians of the Islamic Revolution," also called Sepah or Pasdaran. It is a multi-service primary branch of the Iranian Armed Forces. It was founded by Ruhollah Khomeini and formally organized as a military branch in April 1979 in the aftermath of the Islamic Revolution. The IRGC's constitutional mandate is to ensure the integrity of the Islamic Republic, preventing foreign interference in Iran, thwarting coups by the traditional military, and crushing "deviant movements" that harm the ideological legacy of the Islamic Revolution. At the time this book is written, the IRGC is designated as a terrorist organization by Bahrain, Saudi Arabia, and the United States.

In many countries, ministerial service by young adults is mandatory. In Israel, all citizens over the age of eighteen are required to serve in the Israeli Defense Force (IDF) if they're Jewish, Druze, or Circassian, for a minimum of 12-24 months. They are paid a "subsistence cost," which comes out to less than minimum wage and may be considered "pocket money," but not enough to live on as a salary. The purpose is to protect the state of Israel from outside interference and to preserve the Jewish state. While it is mandatory service for men and women, families are not surprised or manipulated into sending their children for service. But in countries like Iran and even back during Saddam's time in Iraq, ministerial service is mandatory. But the soldiers are the property of the government. As a relative, attempting to seek out information about your loved one typically results in incorrect information or deliberate misinformation.

About three weeks later, Payam's mother came to our house and knocked on the door. My mother and stepfather answered the door, and Payam's parents told them that Payam had been killed by a landmine. The next day, his parents had to go and claim his body and begin preparing for his funeral. The preparation for a Muslim funeral is different than what you might typically expect here in the United States. Muslims don't keep the body in the morgue for days, and there is no embalming, so the body must be buried quickly. Muslims believe in the "dust to dust" concept, so they avoid the process of embalming, which preserves the body. The body is also not dressed up, and nothing is applied to the hair or face. The body is washed and prepared in a room with ceramic tile, then placed on a marble block by the immediate family. As you can imagine, preparing the body of your beloved son or nephew after being blown up by a land mine was a gruesome sight. The body is wrapped in a white sheet, and prayers are offered over the body of the deceased. There are no open caskets, so funerals are burial and memorial services only.

I questioned what happened to my friend and struggled to understand what would happen to him now that he had passed away. Did he go to Heaven? His story was repeated for families all over the country. All over Iran, families were forced to cleanse and bury their broken and deceased family members and then cover the costs of the funeral expenses. The economy in Iran had suffered a severe impact from the Revolution and the war with Iraq. The suffering throughout the country was great and became part of their identity as the years passed. The government used the photographs of the soldiers as martyrs and coined them "holy warriors" when really, they were just children, forced to fight for a new government that needed a frontline to preserve their agenda. There were murals and photograph galleries in public buildings, schools, and neighborhoods. Members of the United States military can attest to the martyrdom and physical displays of photographs and memorial shrines all over the Middle East and many other countries around the world. It's living proof of a family's sacrifice for the greater good of a country in political and religious turmoil. Families are led to believe that losing their loved ones will lead to a paradise that is better than their current existence on Earth.

Hadith: (n.) a collection of traditions containing sayings of the prophet Muhammad which, with accounts of his daily practice (the Sunna), constitute the major source of guidance for Muslims.

In some parts of the Islamic world, kids and those who are uneducated are told that if they lose their life in a holy war or Jihad, they'll get the reward of 72 virgins in Paradise. It is in reference to a weak Hadith that is taken out of context by extremists who manipulate the uneducated masses. Imagine a boy in the Middle East who lives in a culture where casual dating is forbidden, and his tribal cultural desire would be to get married and have a family, being told he will have 72 wives. The thought process they go through must be one of a rewarding dream come true. These corrupted religious trainings convince young boys and men who have never experienced sex with a woman that if they blow themselves up, they will be rewarded with many virgins in paradise. Have you ever heard of a ghost having an erection? Yeah, me neither. But somehow, this kind of thinking is duplicated over and over amongst extremist groups who use cultural influences, guilt trips, and corrupted interpretations of religious texts to recruit and brainwash many who have no background in the theological aspects of religious teachings. Luckily, even though I was subjected to some of the twisted teachings at school, I had a family in my life who would set the record straight when I would ask about things I was being taught at the training camps.

When it comes to Hadiths, they should have a chain of narration that is verified by religious scholars. Hadith is used to teach the correct application of what was said and/or practiced by Muhammad, which is to be verified for authenticity, preventing it from being taken out of context, and yet it still happens all around the world. A hadith that is weak and has a loose chain of verification by scholars is referred to as "*Gharib hadith*," meaning it's unverified and may not be applied to a Muslim's way of life. While the Quran is the recitation of the words Muhammad received through the Angel Gabriel as it was delivered to him by the God of Abraham to spread to the descendants of Ismael (Arabs), the Hadith is the formative example of the prophet's life application for mankind to follow. A good example would be that the Jews read the Torah, the Old Testament. The Talmud is the central text for rabbinic Judaism. It is the Jewish law for cultural life. It is how Moses applied those laws and how Jewish families, to this day, follow with their own application of that holy guidance.

For those readers who work in law enforcement, you are familiar with the term "chain of custody" and the reliability of evidence necessary in court cases. If evidence is tarnished or weak, it would be too easy to manipulate the situation and alter the outcome of the course proceedings. It's the same deal with Hadith – the information must be verified as true before it can be righteously applied to one's daily life. So, then one has to wonder if those teachers are really Muslim. Are they corrupting Islam by ignoring what the Quran really says and instead opting for a flawed interpretation of the religious applications in weak Hadith?

According to the Quran, Christians and Jews are "the people of the Book," the *Ahlul Kitab,* so why are so many extremist groups against Christians, Jews, and the countries that are majority Christians and Jews? Are they following the Quran or their own personal mission? This issue has influenced wars, with politicians and world leaders taking a stand, one way or another. Even a father who ran over his own daughter committed an atrocity according to the Quran, but those who have a warped take on Islam will find a way to justify his actions in order to save their personal standing in the community.

After Payam's death, many in our community began to question if losing those we loved was actually the better deal and how that would impact us when it was our turn to bury our dead. With each passing birthday, the fear over my own life increased for myself and my family.

Chapter 7
Traditions and Honor Killings

I've shared stories about how family-oriented and loving Middle Easterners can be, but they can also carry emotional baggage and extreme personality traits too. There are generational cycles in every culture, but in the Middle East, you can't hold onto the victimhood mentality like some do here in the United States. You have two options overseas: you can learn from those around you and decide to do better while getting out of the negative cycle, or you fall into the same routine as the generation before you and are doomed to repeat it for your own children. Sometimes, an adolescent or teen decides they want out of whatever family dynamic they feel is negative or holding them back. It may be deciding to study at university or to date someone outside of their nationality or religion, or even to date at all against the parents' wishes.

From a young age, children are taught lessons that are meant for protection but also to preserve the child's reputation well into adulthood. "Don't wear that – what will people think of you…or, more importantly, us as your parents?!" "Don't behave like that – only loose and fast girls act like that." "Don't go out without your cousins; even then, be home early. Only kids that get into trouble are out running around." "Don't hang around with that girl. Everybody knows she's a slut, and they'll assume you are one too." "That boy is dating a girl from a different religion. Don't get any ideas because we won't tolerate that in this family." There are so many examples, most of them we can laugh about now as adults, but for many families, it's not a joke and can be a matter of life and death.

The actions of the individual impacts the family as a whole, and especially the parents. It's not just about promiscuity or dating outside of one's culture – it can be additional pressure to get good grades or help out at home or get a job and help the family financially. Many families in the Middle East struggle to put food on the table, and the youth feel a heavy burden compared to more privileged countries where a teen's responsibilities may be to focus on school and some chores on the weekend. So imagine growing up as I did, with the religious expectation to live up to the legacy of being a Seyed, then becoming trained as a child soldier, along with my family's expectations as I grew up and established a career and business.

Reflecting back on my own expectations and obligations, I'm reminded of a day when we were outside with my classmates and friends, waiting for school to begin, and we saw a young woman high up in a building looking out of the window. She was wearing a headscarf (*roosari* or *hijab*) and looked like she was cleaning the windows, but before I or anyone else around me knew what was happening, she jumped and hit the ground in plain view. The impact of her fall made the headscarf come loose, and her brain matter was all over the place on those of us standing near her and the ground around us. Her body was mangled and splayed in an awkward manner. It was a horrific and gruesome sight, which many seasoned adults couldn't handle, let alone a bunch of kids who were stunned, revolted, and scared all at once. All I remember after that is passing out and waking up in the principal's office. It was too much for my young brain to handle. Someone had cleaned up the blood and body matter that had hit me when the woman jumped, but when I stood up to go to class, I saw part of her brain tissue still stuck to one of my shoes. Let's just say I couldn't eat for a few days. That image is forever embedded in my mind. I've seen it time and time again when, as a cop, I would go to a shooting, car wreck, or a suicide, where the victim had severe head injuries. I guess my tolerance level had been maxed out by the time I got into police work because seeing folks' brains all over the place wasn't affecting me much at all. Except when it was a young child that had been killed in a car wreck. That kind of sight has always affected me differently.

I remember, in January of 1995, I was still in my field training program, riding with a sergeant in a small town in central Texas. It was around 9 PM when we were dispatched to a corner house in a rich neighborhood of the city I worked in. A passerby had driven by the house and saw what appeared to be someone lying on the ground in the driveway near the garage door. I'm not sure why they didn't stop to check on the person, but at least they called it in. It was a cold night, about 28 degrees, which is very odd in Texas. Within four minutes, my FTO (Tim) and I arrived at the scene. He was driving, and when we pulled into the driveway, the headlights illuminated the ground, I could clearly see an old man lying face up in the driveway and in a pool of blood. In his right hand, he had a small .38 caliber revolver. As I got out of the passenger side, Tim told me not to walk near the body. The man was clearly dead. The large pool of blood covered about a two-foot area around his head, and because the ground was so cold, the blood had coagulated about an inch and a half thick.

Tim called on the radio for a detective to be dispatched. We worked in a small town of only eleven officers, including the chief. The detective, who was also a Lieutenant, lived two doors down from where I lived. So, I knew he would be there within a few minutes. As we waited, Tim used the police caution tape and taped off the driveway. While he was securing the scene, I couldn't help wondering why the man had shot himself. His wife, who was inside the home, had no clue. We hadn't been there for three or four minutes before an elderly woman came out of the door that was inside the garage and commenced to scream at the top of her lungs. Tim stopped what he was doing and ran towards her to get her off the scene. This was for two reasons: One would be to make sure she didn't touch anything, and second, to minimize the trauma that she would be facing and experiencing.

As he walked her back into the house, I looked at the top part of the garage door frame, and I could see a splatter of dark spots and a bullet hole. It appeared the old man had sat Indian style in the driveway, near the open garage door, and shot himself once in the head through the mouth. I could see the brain matter on the ground. I know! You read this and picture yourself being there. Imagining the thoughts that would be going through your head. I was too! The smell that was present is something that cannot be put into words. Those who have experienced being present after a traumatic violent death can attest to the odd feeling and smell that is present. I was standing less than five feet from the body and could smell and feel the thickness of the dense atmosphere. I had seen and felt this before when I was a kid growing up in the Middle East.

I remembered one instance when I was eight years old, walking to school in Iran, and I watched a group of the "new military" personnel stop their Land Cruiser and approach a man who was walking about thirty feet in front of me. I am not sure what they said to him, but within four seconds, one of them raised his rifle and blew the guy's head off directly in front of me. Now remember, I was eight years old at the time. I saw the head explode from the high-caliber rifle round, and the man dropped to the ground. His brain matter splattered all over the sidewalk. I instantly felt and smelled the same exact thing I was experiencing on that call. It was a situation that had been embedded forever in my brain. And I can only attribute my calm reaction to the suicide call to situations like that when I was a child. I had seen so much death that it almost made me emotionless. To this day, it has the same effect. Conditioning and experiences in life do affect how someone reacts to situations, I suppose.

Going back to the lady who had committed suicide by jumping off the building, I can only assume that she was feeling trapped or may have done something that brought a negative outlook on her or her family. The pressures of her family's expectations must have become too much for her to bear, so her solution was to crash into the pavement in front of strangers and even children as her final message to her loved ones. Other young women take matters into their own hands, like a Romeo and Juliet story, when they were forbidden to see a boyfriend or were denied the possibility of marrying someone her parents didn't approve of...and others were killed by the very fathers, brothers, cousins or uncles that professed to do it "for her own good." The reality is that a young girl's actions reflected on them as the men of the family, as if her actions were a sign that they couldn't control or lead their family down the right path, which resulted in her promiscuity or reckless behavior. I guess they never heard that "forbidden fruit tastes so much sweeter," where a forbidden relationship seems so much more passionate and exciting, especially when you're young and one big walking hormone.

There are so many rules, many of them arbitrary, when it comes to religion and the purity of lineage, not just for countries in the Middle East but also Asia, Africa, and others. Some experts say that purity of race is becoming rare in many parts of the world because of interracial relationships, and most certainly inter-religious relationships too. A tribal society will want to protect its lineage and protecting the reputation of the family is included in that type of mentality. They consent to certain marriages because they know the family and trust that the daughter is pure and the son is of noble character and able to provide for the bride and future offspring. Honor killings happen more often in villages in Afghanistan or Northern Africa because the tribal lifestyle still exists to this day. Even when some families move to Western countries, they bring that mentality with them, even when Western laws do not allow you to discipline or even kill, despite one's personal convictions. There are family men from many foreign countries who are in prison today because they did what they thought was their duty or obligation to the family, even as far as killing a beloved daughter simply because she spoke to a male classmate on the phone about homework or walked around the park with her teenage crush.

In some countries, there is a hierarchy within the society, referred to as a caste system, where individuals are not permitted to marry someone above or below their level in society. This also has to do with some respective religions because they believe that inter-religious marriages will break down the lineage within one religion or the other. Sometimes the religion is passed down from the father's side, other times from the mother's side. So what happens when you marry a father-dominant religion to a mother-dominant religion? Chaos, that's what – because every family gathering and birth of a new child will create a reminder of the very beginning of this marital union! Life in the Middle East isn't like it is here in the West. Societies abroad are much slower at pushing progressive ideologies and acceptance outside the norm, especially with regard to the core of society, which is the family unit.

In 2007, I went against family tradition when marrying the Palestinian Christian woman I met in Mississippi. Neither of us got our parents' permission, even though we were independently living on our own and practically middle-aged. When I finally told my mom, there was an awkward silence on her end of the phone. "What are you thinking? We don't marry Arabs!" was the next thing out of her mouth. Come to think of it, I never sought input from my parents prior to getting married the first time, either. I guess my assimilation had sunk in by then! Marrying an Iranian of another religion or even an American was more tolerable or understandable than marrying an Arab. Being Arab was the issue, not that she was a Christian. Arabs and Iranians have a deeply rooted animosity towards each other that dates back to ancient times. We're kind of like oil and vinegar. We don't really blend well, but people love us mixed together in a salad!

The family is strong in cultures around the world, but in many Middle Eastern countries, especially those dealing with serious economic strife, it is acceptable and understandable to endure manipulation, extortion, and exploitation in order to protect and feed one's family. Sometimes a family member gets into trouble, and the only way out is to become involved on the government or police's behalf. The individual may be manipulated and forced to carry out a "tax" on another country in order to accomplish a bigger goal and save his family from harm or ruin their reputation. This individual could be sent to another country in order to be used as a suicide bomber. The family can now look at their loved one as a martyr, while for the government, this individual's life held no real significance when focused on the greater goal. In Iran, they use Afghanis or Arabs to police their citizens. When Iranian citizens are attacked by what seems like their own people, it's actually imported Afghanis, Lebanese, or Iraqis. It's easier for those with no interpersonal connections who don't speak the same language or know the family when trying to arrest a young girl and her classmates on the street or arresting a father coming out of a store with his little boy. Iranian extremists don't blow themselves up, but they have no problem getting someone else to do the dirty work. Using folks from other countries will allow them to feel as though their own hands are clean – plausible deniability. Some Arabs won't blow themselves up, but they might see no issue with manipulating a Pakistani to do it.

To understand the individual, you must understand their background, culture, religion, and the family that raised him or her. The clues are there, like an onion, as we peel back the layers to reach the core of the person who thinks and moves through society with good or bad intentions.

Chapter 8
Muezzin

Muezzin (n.): a man who calls Muslims to prayer from the minaret of a mosque. Friday prayers are called "adhan" for public worship. The call to daily prayer which is five times a day at dawn, noon, mid-afternoon, sunset, and nightfall is called "salat."

I was about eleven years old when I was selected by religious teachers at my school to be the *muezzin* on a Friday. As a Seyed, it was an honor and a privilege that only those with this lineage would receive, so I knew it was a big deal. Remember, I shared earlier how I was taught from a young age that certain religious practices and obligations were non-negotiables. I was proud of my religious identity and wanted to make my family proud too.

Muharram is the first month of the Islamic calendar. It's a time when warfare is forbidden in the Muslim world. The tenth day of the month is Ashura. I spent several weeks in singing lessons and meetings with scholars to practice for my Friday debut. This prayer call can be heard for several miles, and I needed to be strong and skilled. I would be reciting the Adhan (call for prayer), kind of like churches ringing the bell for their services, only mine would be in a prayer song.

Ashura is the day of commemoration in Islam among Shia Muslims. It is observed through large demonstrations of high-scale mourning as it marks the death of Husayn ibn Ali, who was beheaded during the Battle of Karbala in 680 C.E. For Sunni Muslims, Ashura is observed through celebratory fasting, as it marks the day of salvation for Moses and the Israelites, who successfully escaped from Biblical Egypt after Moses called upon God's power to part the Red Sea.

Now, most people who know me will agree that I am vertically challenged. Now imagine me as a kid – yup, I was even shorter! I was also a chubby kid who loved to eat. Lots of people eat *khoresht- e-gheimeh,* which is a Persian stew, on Ashura, and my stomach was full. You know that bloated feeling that hurts so good when you ate more than you should have but just couldn't stop because you were enjoying it so much? That was me then, waddling my way up a narrow, windy staircase, much like the interior of a lighthouse, in order to reach the top to do the prayer call. It was a tight squeeze as I maneuvered my way up, anxious and excited at the same time. There were marches, people were reciting prayers, and money was donated to buy food to feed thousands of people. Their Golden Corral was *khoresht gheimeh.* If you know, you know! The food and festivities were just one aspect of the holiday, however. Many in attendance were there to commemorate the torture and beheading of Hussain at the Battle of Karbala. This was a massive-scale, highly-skilled mourning to relive the historical event where people mimicked the pain and suffering that Hussain endured. They would slap their chests while chanting, and others would practice self-flagellation by using chains to whip their own backs as they paraded through the area. Blood stained the clothes of those who practiced in such a way while onlookers chanted along, prayed, or socialized. Even though many chose to uphold tradition in this manner, certain groups have variations on how this day is commemorated.

We attended the Masjid Seyed, a mosque in Isfahan, but cities around the country, as well as Muslims from other parts of the world, all have their own take on the original event. I still feel the tingling of pain in my back as I remember my own participation as a child, knowing I was obligated to do as others did in the massive assembly. Sometimes as a child, we sense the pressure and expectations to follow suit even if we may have preferred to stand by and only observe. If you didn't partake in the process, you or your family would be seen as against the religion or community or, even more importantly, against the new government. I was a kid, following along with the traditions and actions that were part of this special day. After about half an hour of alternating the chains over my left, then right shoulder, I had blisters and cut marks that allowed the blood to seep through my shirt. Even to this day, when I see a parade televised, I can still feel the pain in my back as if it's happening again. We suffered bruises, scabs that took weeks to heal, burning, and itching as the skin became sensitive. Most kids can't even handle a paper cut, let alone self-flagellation! But you had to go along or feel like you were going against your people and what everybody else did, you must do too. Remember, as a child, we didn't ask questions, argue back, and certainly didn't have the luxury of "opting out."

The ritual practices aren't always the same in every sect of Islam. There are factions of Shias in Iraq and Pakistan who go too far with self-flagellation. Some groups actually use a knife to cut slits on their skull and even the skull of infant children. But these subsects are not always well received by more traditional members of a sect as a whole. As I said earlier, the rituals of every subsect varies in Islam, as it does in every other world religion. Christianity has its own variations. Under the Orthodox school of thought, there are variations of ritual practices and doctrines, and the same exists in the protestant sect. The same goes for Judaism. Many see a religion as a unified set of beliefs and practices, not realizing that in all religions, rituals change based on the location, culture, and other factors that affect belief. We have the same here in the States. As a Christian, one would look at groups like the Branch Davidians, Westboro Baptist Church, and many others as not following the true teachings of Jesus Christ as it doesn't coincide with their beliefs. You can see that any religion can be interpreted based on what someone wants it to be for them. Hence, it's always best to go to the root and be familiarized with the beginning to help understand how things progressed with that religion. Judaism, Christianity, and Islam are the three largest religions in the world. Each has many variations, depending on where it's practiced and how it's interpreted. Imagine how a religion that was introduced to Arabs in the seventh century can be affected when interpreted by members of tribes that have such deep-rooted cultural beliefs. Now imagine how it can be manipulated and used as a way to literally influence the minds of those following it.

Chapter 9
The Escape

When I was fourteen years old, my stepdad and mom were dressed up one day and getting the courtyard *"hayyat"* ready for guests. A *"mehmooni"* could be anything from a few friends coming over for casual tea and dessert or a full multi-course meal with dancing and twenty to forty people. Middle Easterners don't often wait for a yearly occasion or even a milestone such as a birthday, for example, and they will throw a party or invite guests over just to celebrate the end of the week or show off a new Persian rug.

My typical question as a fourteen-year-old seeing them dressed up was, "Who's coming over?" My stepfather's friend from Tehran worked for the *Majless,* which was like the legislative assembly or city council. They were planning a strategy to get me out of Iran before I was drafted into war at fifteen. I found out that my mother had been talking to my father's sisters to persuade my father, through the grapevine, to assist in the master plan. She would never think to call and discuss directly with my father. With existing animosity on his part and the sense of pride and modesty on her part, it was best to apply the art of guilt and influence via his sisters in appealing to my father's primary concern over his reputation, less so the concern over his son's safety. How guilty do you think a man would feel if he didn't step up to help and his only son went off to war, only to be blown up by a land mine within a few short weeks? Exactly. Thus, the master plan was born.

Middle Easterners have a concept called "*tarof,*" which is difficult to translate because, as far as I know, there isn't an adequate word that exists in the English language. It can be described as an offer, a rebuttal of resistance (even if you really do want the thing they are offering), and then an insistence, then an acceptance. For example, if you go to someone's house, you cannot go empty-handed. You must bring the host a dessert, flowers, or some other gift. The host then insists that you "shouldn't have." (But they'll complain later after the party if you don't bring anything!) They will then serve the food you got, and you will resist and decline the offer, saying it was for the hosts to enjoy. The host then insists again and offers more options to you, asking you to please partake. This can sometimes go back and forth several times before you, the guest, finally give in and accept. In this scenario, if you accepted the first offer, it would give the impression that you brought the dessert (or whatever it was) only so you could eat it yourself or that you weren't properly fed at home and only came to their house to be fed by the hosts. It's not a good look. *Taroff* can also be the game of back and forth of the restaurant bill or taking a group of kids out to the movies, which parent will pay for the group, and so on. A personal budget may be an issue for some, but in that case, the individual will simply decline to be in that situation to begin with. If you don't have the budget for the *taroff,* especially if you intend to "win," then you stay home!

I hoped my father would help me travel to the United States and take me into his home. Most flights from Iran are predominantly to Europe, Turkey, or Dubai, UAE. In my case, Turkey was the decided route where my father would meet me, and we would travel together back to the US. They came up with a fictitious medical diagnosis and received approval for medical treatments abroad. On a hot summer day, we traveled from Isfahan to Tehran to go to the Swiss Embassy. The only way I could get my passport updated as an American citizen then was through the Swiss Embassy. The last time I had a passport, I was a baby, so it needed to be renewed with an updated photograph. I remember the tall, blonde, blue-eyed woman at the embassy who spoke fluent Farsi and her other native languages. I think it's the same sense of wonder and confusion when people see me and see what they assume is a Hispanic or Middle Eastern man, and when I speak, I can sound like I'm from the deep swamps of Louisiana or the dusty ranches of the Great State of Texas. It's a mind trip for sure!

Turkey was the safer choice, but it would still be a three to six-month process until my passport was ready and I was cleared for travel. We were driven by a private car back home to Isfahan. The driver was Kurdish, and having learned of our plan, he offered a smuggling opportunity to assist in our travel plans. Many Kurds were making their way through the Middle East to safer territories and were well-versed in smuggling families and individuals through various terrains and security checkpoints. He also offered a "*dua*," a prayer for easy solutions, and a challenge-free plan for my travel to the United States. You know, it's kind of funny when I reflect on my law enforcement career as an anti-smuggling expert and realize the tone was set way back when I was smuggled myself!

When we arrived home, my mother told me I needed to call my father and update him on the plan's details. I hadn't spoken to him in so many years, so to say I was hesitant knowing it would be an awkward phone call was an understatement. Nevertheless, I made the call and told him to plan to meet me in Turkey when I would have my passport and be ready to complete the travel to the U.S. I learned later that my mother and stepfather invested the equivalent of $750,000 for a bribe to secure approval for medical treatments abroad. Corruption and extortion were and continue to be commonplace in the Middle East. Money bought freedom, assets, law enforcement, and intelligence cooperation.

On a Wednesday, several weeks later, we received the letter of approval for me to leave. I had two days to prepare for my trip. It finally hit me that I would probably never see Iran again. I didn't know then, but I wouldn't see my mother again until 2009, over two decades later. My mother was very stoic, repeating that "it was all in the hands of God." I will never quite understand the emotions she must have felt over my leaving. She wanted her only child to survive, but that also meant she had to lose me to a new land far away. Many mothers throughout history made similar choices, but it doesn't change the significant impact it has on the mother and child.

There were 48 hours of chaos with paperwork, packing, and verbal preparation. My mother and stepfather reviewed privacy instructions and government tracking strategies to make me more aware of my surroundings and behaviors. Any individual who went against the control and dictatorship of the current regime was thought to be "waging war against God," even for the slightest offense. As this book is being written, we are currently seeing many Iranian citizens being arrested, beaten, raped, and murdered by the Regime forces, and their crime is a broad category, even if it's just too much hair showing from under a head scarf *"hijab"* or *"roosari"* (head covering).

The new revolution of 2022 began with the arrest and murder-by-beating of Mahsa Amini, who was arrested for "improper headscarf," showing too much of her hair. How much is "too much" is subjective, especially in a country where the front 3-4 inches and bottom 3-4

The Patriot Jihadi

We got my hard copy ticket to Turkey and packed up to drive to Tehran. On the drive, there was a flood of emotions for all of us. Before 9/11, families were still allowed to attend to their loved ones all the way to the terminal gate at the airport. My mother prayed the Ayatul Kursi, one of the best-known verses of the Quran and widely memorized and displayed in the Muslim world. It is often recited *"to ward of jinn"* and any bad energy surrounding a person or an anticipated event. It is also recited by Muslims to grant spiritual or physical protection before setting out on a journey and before going to sleep. Often, there will also be a feast over a sacrificial lamb as well.

My mother was wearing a *"chador,"* which is a loose-fitting full-length overcoat that covers the shape of the body for additional modesty, along with the headscarf. She was containing her emotions because the perception she wanted to convey was that her child was simply going to another country (the equivalent of traveling to another state for a treatment not offered in your home state) and that I would soon return. The importance of maintaining composure overpowered the reality of the "forever" goodbye. We weren't sure if we'd ever see each other again, but the fear of being exposed by our behavior or emotions in an airport full of security personnel was enough to help us remain cognizant of what we conveyed to onlookers.

My stepfather's entire identity was falsified after the onset of the revolution, so standing there with my mother, he was aware of his surroundings as well. "Just a pharmaceutical rep" waiting with his wife as his stepson departs for medical treatments; he showed very little emotion as well, though, by this time, we were both fond of each other and recognized the parting may be the last time we would see each other. I was to board a bus directly to the plane and anxiously said my goodbyes and looked around me as I took my seat on the bus. There was a film of dust on all the bus windows as I observed the individuals who were to be passengers on the same flight, as well as security guards positioned throughout the bus.

The entire time I was on the bus as it taxied out to the plane and coming off the bus to enter the airplane, I kept imagining someone finding out that I was escaping Iran and what would become of my parents or me if someone were to catch us. The flight attendant who greeted me as I entered the airplane was wearing a full *burka*, which covers the majority of the face, an even more extreme version compared to the *"chador"* that my mother was wearing. It was a far cry from the Emirates flight attendants who now wear high heels, pencil skirts, and pillbox hats with a sheer scarf draped softly around a full face of makeup and accessories. The flight attendant in the burka told me where to sit, and the Regime's soldiers on board did a final security check before the plane was permitted to take off. I was wearing a *"Zulfiqar"* necklace, which is a pendant made in the shape of a sword with a split tip.

Zulfiqar: "fiqar" means "splitter or differentiator," the vertebrae of the back, the bones of the spine, which are set in regular order, one upon the other" which can be said of the notches, grooves or indentations on the sword, but also the two points of the tip of the sword. It is often invoked in talismans. Legend has it that Muhammad asked God to give him a sword. The sword appeared in Muhammad's hands and then Muhammad throws the sword to Ali to replace his old broken sword.

One of the soldiers eyed my necklace, and seeing it as a religious symbol of my religious lineage, he gave me a nod and continued checking the fuselage. The inspections were completed, and they ordered the door to the airplane closed. Only then was I able to take a huge sigh of relief and began to relax my body. Then, the realization of leaving my homeland finally hit me, and the emotions of leaving my mother for what I thought would be forever. I was "almost there," yet my life's journey had barely begun.

Chapter 10
Hard Landing

The flight to Turkey was filled with thoughts about my transition to a new country and many unknowns. The flight from Iran to Turkey wasn't too long, so when the plane landed, I was ready to see a new country for the first time. There were still some women who wore various degrees of body and hair coverings, but most of the women there did not cover in public. There were no soldiers with guns milling about and no government officials at every turn. I looked around anxiously for my father and saw all the airport signage written in Turkish or English. I spotted my father, a short and stout man with hair that can only be described as "Chia pet hair." If you aren't familiar with the novelty home-grown miniature grassy plant, his hair was bigger than life and very puffy for his diminutive stature. "*Shaheen jan*" (Shaheen, dear) was the first thing he said to me as we greeted each other. We walked through the airport in Ankara, Turkey, which was very Western in style compared to what I had just experienced in Iran. Beautiful mosques and architecture are all over Turkey, rich with culture and remnants of the Ottoman Empire.

I began seeing flags from other countries in the airport and spotted "Old Glory," the American flag. It gave me a sense of safety and comfort in knowing I was almost completely free. I was almost home. After he picked me up from the airport, we went straight to the US Embassy in Turkey to pick up my American passport. We made our way to the parking lot where my father had rented a four-door Audi to drive us to Istanbul. We stayed in a hotel on the European side where we would then drive to Amsterdam. Apparently, my father had secured great airfare for flights on KLM to Atlanta, Georgia; his seat in first class, mine in economy. We drove for two days to get to Amsterdam, including hotel, food, and rest stops.

We finally arrived for our flight in Amsterdam, I only knew a few key phrases in English, one of which was "Hello, I would like one Coke, please." When I boarded the plane and got settled, every time the flight attendant said anything to me, that's what I repeated. The flight to Atlanta took about eight and a half hours, with me drinking Coke after Coke. I didn't even consider that there would be a bathroom on the airplane! I had never flown before, and at almost fifteen years old, I experienced tons of new things in a short time. By the time we landed, all I could think of was needing to use the restroom. I quickly found my father and asked him for the nearest toilet, and he pointed in the general direction of the restrooms. I ran into the first doorway I saw and immediately found a bathroom stall to relieve my bulging bladder. The automatic flusher scared me, as we didn't have standard toilets like that in Iran. After experimenting with the flusher and realizing that there wasn't anyone watching me pee and flushing for me, I realized these Western restrooms were quite an experience! While washing my hands, I heard a sound from the other side of the wall partition. Curious as I was, I peeked my head around the corner and saw a woman washing her hands on the other side. I quickly said, "Hello!" and then ran out. I found my dad and asked him about the urinals and toilets I had just seen. He chuckled and realized all this was new for me, so he took me back into the restroom for a quick tour of the Western amenities. I also realized I had mistakenly entered the women's restroom in my hurry to find a toilet!

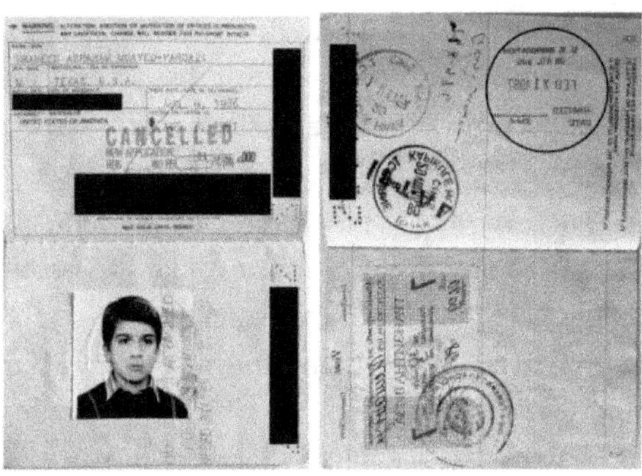

We then drove from Atlanta to his home in Alabama. I met my stepmother, Sue, and after traveling for days and being a generally stinky fourteen-year-old boy, she got me settled and suggested I take a much-needed shower. Iranians at the time were generally very clean, especially with regard to toilet hygiene, but the concept of showering daily was not a typical thing for Iranians like it is for Americans. This started my assimilation into American society. Our first shopping trip was to K-Mart to buy essentials I would need for school. The house was spacious and had a large television with a satellite dish. I had bacon, grits, and scrambled eggs for breakfast for the first time. My father quickly began to force me to assimilate into the American way of life, especially concerning dropping my religious tendencies, like not eating pork products. He seemed to have an agenda of forcing me to eat pork products when I clearly tried to avoid eating certain foods, even if my stepmother tried to provide alternatives. I was in survival mode and didn't expect care and kindness, especially from him. I didn't take things he did or said personally, and in hindsight, I believe the anger and resentment towards my mother leaving him led to those feelings being projected onto me as well. He met his obligation to get me out of Iran, but he wasn't going to do me any favors by being loving or accommodating any more than providing a roof over my head.

I started high school and began learning English. I heard new music for the first time, and bands like "Motley Crue" became my favorite. I wasn't allowed to make friends outside of school and was not allowed to partake in extracurricular activities.

My first Christmas in America was in Cullman, Alabama. The family and I went to the annual Christmas parade in town, and I saw men on horses wearing white robes and hoods. It was such an unusual sight, and I asked my stepmother what and who they were, thinking this was another American costume tradition like I had seen for Halloween. She simply said, "Those folks don't like people like you..." and quickly turned the conversation to something else. I thought it was an odd state-ment to make because I wondered, "How can they not like me when they don't even know me?" It wasn't until years later that I learned about the Ku Klux Klan, but interestingly, certain demographics in the South are very similar to Middle Easterners or other minorities in general. If you know anything about ancient Persian culture, research the Aryan race.

It helped me out in many different instances, and it's inter-esting. I'd get into the whole Aryan topic, but you'll have to wait on another book for that!

There was a tornado in the town where we lived, and we suffered significant damage, so we moved to Decatur when I started tenth grade. I heard the symphony band practice and was in awe of the drums. I wanted to play the drums and asked to be in the band, so I told my stepmother, who was encouraging and helped me navigate my schedule so my father wouldn't find out. For weeks I practiced at school, learning from the other drum-mers, and surprised my band teacher with how determined I was to learn and master different drums. In a short time, I had exceeded his expectations. I was on fire, passionate about playing, and focused on achieving my goal. This same work ethic and drive have been part of my personality my entire life.

One day, my father came home early when I was at band practice. My stepmother struggled to cover for me, but my father got in his car and drove to the school to find me. He found me in the band room practicing, slammed his way through the door, grabbed me, and dragged me out. He hit me so hard in the face, my nose felt like it exploded. There was so much blood all over me and the hallway, and I wasn't sure it would ever stop. He yelled that I disobeyed him, and luckily the band teacher came out and called the school security and administrators. They took me to the office and told him he had to leave the premises. My father was a well-known physician in the area and had many local connections at the time. While in the school office, they asked me if there was anyone they could call because they feared for my safety if I was to return home without an alternate living arrangement. They called my mother's brother in Houston, Texas, and he arranged for me to move out there with his family immediately.

My uncle's family was warm and welcoming. I stayed with him for a few months until my uncle rented an apartment for me and got me settled in. I started working and used a bicycle to get around. After graduating high school, I worked full-time in a restaurant owned by local Iranians, where I mixed in with Texas natives, Hispanic employees, and a diverse crowd of patrons. I learned to balance my spending on new American fashions while budgeting for my bills and setting aside some as savings. I began meeting my neighbors in the building where I lived and soon learned that one of my neighbors was a police officer. He described what he did for a living and offered to take me on a ride-along. Little did I know, I was about to change the trajectory of my life with one ride in a squad car.

Chapter 11
No Judging

When I graduated from high school, I had already been living on my own in a rented apartment not far from my uncle and his family in Houston, Texas. My English had greatly improved by then, but there were still some circumstances where the slang or context tested my fluency. I definitely still had an accent, but making more friends and working day and night helped me assimilate and enjoy life as a young adult.

At the restaurant where I worked, most employees were Mexican. So, as I was fine-tuning my English, I started to learn Spanish as well, which would come in handy later in my career as I dealt with Mexican Cartel members. I began to learn the dynamics of being a true Texan, which is very different from my beginnings of Southern culture in Alabama. For one, the accent is different, so I'd mix my accents and not only confuse the person I was speaking with, but sometimes I'd confuse myself too! The cooks and busboys only spoke Spanish, and the servers only spoke Texan English. I'm short, so being in Texas and having brown skin made me fit right in with the Mexicans.

While I have always been able to understand both written and oral language, throughout my work life, I've always strived to communicate in a professional yet easy manner so everyone, regardless of their background, can understand – think "Reader's Digest" version! Over the years, students who have attended my classes have offered feedback that reflects my very direct approach to teaching and an easy-to-understand methodology.

As I went through the process of learning to assimilate and how the American way of life should be, I decided to try to enahnce the process by dressing in what was fashionable at the time. I wore Cavariccis and took cues from the show Miami Vice. I listened to Milli Vanilli and all the greatest 80s and 90s hits. I also bought the hottest shoes on the market and learned the hard way that keeping up with your buddies doesn't always leave room for paying rent. My uncle was understanding and gracious in bailing me out, but he also knew it was time to teach me the art of saving and spending so that I wouldn't be short each month. I learned to budget my income as it came in and to save for bigger goals.

I was in a diverse area of Houston, where I learned that people had various lifestyles, sexual affiliations, and religious and cultural backgrounds. My uncle's wife and children were Iranian Jews, so while their religious practices differed from mine, culturally, we were all entrenched in the traditions and practices we knew from back in Iran. For Iranians, the cultural norms trumped most religious details unless, of course, you were living in Iran post-revolution. Then the mullahs and their ideologies became the only way to think, believe and live as an Iranian, even if you weren't Muslim. If you did practice another religion, it could have cost you your life, and it did prove tragic for many Iranians of other faiths and beliefs over the last several decades.

The Patriot Jihadi

Mullah: (n.) a Muslim educated in Islamic theology and sacred law. The term is used in various parts of the Islamic world as a title attached to the name of a scholar or religious leader.

When I worked at the restaurant, we had guests from all backgrounds and walks of life. I remember a group of gay men who were regulars, and one in particular, was very friendly towards me. I was learning how to discern body language, speech patterns, and how to "read between the lines," so I didn't recognize that there may have been a physical attraction on his part, and to this day, I still can't believe why anyone would find a vertically-challenged brown leprechaun attractive! "Friendly" and "flirting" sound very similar when you're still assimilating to a new country and its ways! I later found out that he liked me, and I just politely smiled and declined his interest, but it didn't occur to me to get offended or question his lifestyle. He was just a human being eating dinner with his friends. I didn't need to think or care about what he did after he left the restaurant. I have always believed that we are not to judge, and I'm not The Creator, either. A lot of people around the world assume that all Middle Easterners are ready to vilify anyone that doesn't agree with them, but that's simply not true. I know Palestinians who regularly break bread with Israeli friends abroad, and here in the US, I also know staunch conservatives who work with and enjoy happy hours with liberals. Just because certain governments have a particular agenda or the media feeds you one perspective doesn't mean folks are out hatin' on everybody who disagrees with them. In many homes, we can still have passionate debates with differing opinions and still leave hugging, kissing, and wishing each other well until the next time.

My exposure to a variety of people with different levels of religious connection, cultural backgrounds, sexual affiliations, and languages prepared me for my law enforcement career, where I was able to effectively and objectively investigate possible criminal activity based on facts rather than personal ideologies and biases. Early on, I learned that not everyone is going to be my best friend or even someone I may cross paths with again, but in those moments with a person, I stuck to the facts and the present situation. Contrary to popular belief, it *is* possible to show empathy and neutrality without allowing personal biases or profiling to influence your interactions with others, whether on the job or in your personal life.

Chapter 12
The Blue Line

When I was living in Houston, working at the restaurant, I was living a content life. My neighbor was a police officer, and I began to get curious about his profession and what it entailed. I've always been interested in people, and it seemed that my neighbor had the perfect career for seeing people in all sorts of scenarios, good and bad, and everything in between. I didn't worry about the safety aspect of his job because, in my mind, based on my upbringing and social education in Iran as a child, death was in the hands of God and God alone. He offered to take me on a ride-along, and I loved it.

I was hooked. I began considering a possible career in law enforcement and then paid out-of-pocket to join the local police academy. Once I graduated, one of the staff at the academy became chief in a small city, and the opportunity popped up to have me move two hours away from Houston. Life was full of unknowns, but I began working with a passion and a curiosity that filled my days and nights with new experiences. I was wearing a uniform again, and reflecting on my childhood in Iran, where we idolized men in uniform, I had a sense of pride in my uniform and the practices involved in being a police officer.

Never mind that I was a leprechaun, so the standard 30 L wasn't working for me. I needed 27, so my uniforms always needed to be hemmed! To me, the uniform symbolized strength and protection. I felt a sense of spiritual purpose as well. As a Seyed, serving God means serving humanity. I knew I was destined for a life of service. I was going to fulfill my own personal desire to excel in my career while gaining experience and expanding my skill set. I also wanted to meet the expectations and obligations of family, friends, and colleagues – not an easy thing to do, but I have always tried my best!

Not long after I was working patrol, I was attacked and beaten on duty, which required me to be placed on "light duty." Some teens decided to rob a store, but instead, they whooped me like they were beating the new kid on the block. Being a short little midget has its disadvantages, but it sure makes for good stories! On that fateful night, I was driving near one of the local gas stations, which shared the parking lot with a Sonic Drive-In. As I turned the corner at the red light, I saw a man standing in the alleyway, which separated the convenience store from a fried chicken restaurant to its right. The dude was wearing a pair of blue jean overalls and had a black ski mask over his face. Now, it was well over ninety degrees in the middle of the summer. He was definitely not cold, and that wasn't the place to be wearing an outfit made for the mountains of Colorado.

Knowing he was up to no good, I decided to pull into the gas station shopping center, got out of my car, and feeling ten feet tall and bulletproof, I walked up to him and asked him what he was doing. He kept his dead stare into my eyes and never answered. It was one of those awkward situations that you know is about to turn ugly, but you're already there and hope it doesn't go as bad as it could possibly go. As my luck has it, it did. I reached for his right hand and ordered him to turn around so I could pat him down for weapons. Well, he had the idea that since he was taller, he would take control and swung around, popped me with his fist right on the left side of my face and ear, and I fell to the ground. I could hear and see the little birds chirping in my head.

But, the stubborn little dude that I was, I wasn't letting go. He started to run, dragging me like a rag doll as he ran into the Sonic parking lot. There in the parking lot were a bunch of high school kids. Guess what? They decided why not jump in and have a field day. I reach for my radio to call for help, and I quickly realize that on the ride across the parking lot, my radio had come off, and yep, no help would be coming.

In the process of being stomped and beaten with boots, someone had managed to grab my StreamLight SL20 flashlight and went to work on my head. Let's just say those birds I'd been hearing had now become a flock of geese. I was bleeding all over the place, my head was spinning, and all I could think of was, "I ain't letting go of this bastard." During the chaos, with over thirty kids jumping in to get a lick in on the midget cop, I heard a loud horn from what sounded like an 18-wheeler. It was one of the local wrecker drivers, who was a volunteer firefighter and the brother of one of the other cops that worked with me.

He had seen the chaos unfold in a matter of less than a minute and, luckily, had summoned help by calling the dispatch over his fire radio. As I was now pinned between two cars, with other patrons waiting in the stalls at the Sonic, getting their food and watching the mayhem, I heard him yell and start to kick the kids off of me. He grabbed me off the ground, dragged me to the front of his wrecker, and held off the few kids trying to get to me. I remember him telling the few that if they got any closer, he'd "break their necks and shit down their throats." Now mind you, I'm half dizzy, freaked out, can't breathe, and was covered in blood.

The kids ended up running off, and some of the patrons at the Sonic had come to assist the wrecker driver and me. One lady started to wipe the blood off my face and held me up against the bumper of the truck, trying to talk to me. I must have been in and out of consciousness because I only remember bits and pieces.

I can't remember much of what happened next except being loaded into an ambulance and waking up in the emergency room in Bryan, Texas, which would have been at least a 45-minute drive. I don't remember the ride. All I know is I woke up on a bed in a triage room, and my head was pounding as if I had been hit by a train. Heck, I may have been; I just can't remember.

The prognosis was a broken nose, a severe concussion, and two broken ribs. What really pissed me off was that they had cut my duty belt and vest off me, which I had paid for out of pocket. So there went about $1100 out of my pocket. Nowadays, that's not too high, but when I was only making $8.92 per hour as a cop, it was literally a whole month's income after taxes. Yep, that's what the pay was. I think that year and the year after, I grossed around $19,000 on my 1040 EZ form.

Heck, the most I ever made as a cop with 25 years on the job was $23.64 an hour, and that was in 2020. You guessed it, the South doesn't pay cops much, and folks often wonder why they can't get many good candidates. Sure, the general public is mostly supportive of law enforcement since the South is majority conservative, but I guess politicians don't really see cops as public servants who put their lives on the line but rather pawns for political ambitions. You hear a lot of politicians in the southern states talk about how they support law enforcement, but they don't put their money where their mouth is.

What good came out of being on light duty for a few months was that I attended a lot of training. My chief, who was a really good guy, told me that since I couldn't do anything at work, I should find training classes to get some education under my belt. And boy, did that advice really help set me up for later advancements in my career. It didn't help me get any taller, though. I was still the shortest dude in the county wearing a police uniform.

When I was finally back on the job again, my first stop resulted in seizing five kilos of cocaine. I remember on that stop, I reached for the spare tire in the Lincoln Town Car and fell right into the trunk! I was about to arrest the guy driving, but he felt so sorry for me, he helped me out of the trunk before I hauled him to jail. That stop and arrest was my gateway experience into the world of interdiction and what would become my career path well into the future.

What was exciting is that the guy decided to cooperate, and with the help of the DEA, we delivered the coke to Oklahoma City. In that operation, I was introduced to a bigger world beyond my small-town experiences, where I worked alongside federal authorities and learned about the wider world of smuggling operations.

To put it into perspective, it was like a hit of crack cocaine. I was hooked for life. That was my new addiction! I've heard it said that we should never apologize for being ambitious and driven to be passionate about a career we love. Well, that was exactly how I felt – unapologetically chasing that first "high" for the next twenty-five years.

Shawn Pardazi

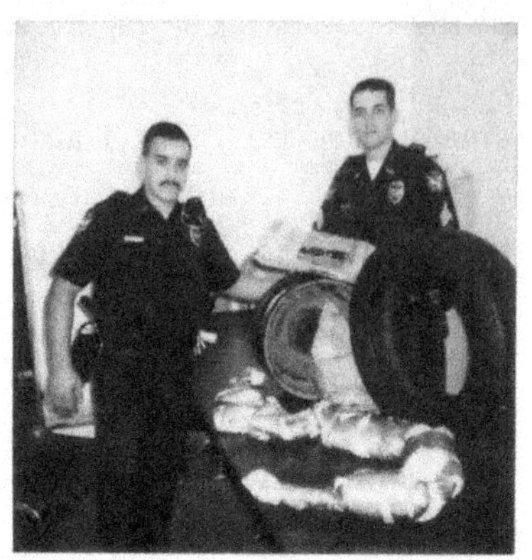

Chapter 13
Blondie

I was working patrol and continuing my education through training as it became available. I was saving money and keeping my head focused on my life and career. Every morning as I was winding down my shift, I'd stop at a local gas station and mini-mart. I had become friendly with the employees there, and a regular customer that came in every morning around the same time started to notice me. I found out she had asked about my situation, and I thought she was cute. We started chatting, and I soon realized she was a single mom with two kids who had been dealt a bad hand with her marriage, or so I thought. I later learned the guy wasn't as bad as I had initially thought, and after witnessing how I treated her, but most importantly, his kids, he grew to respect and appreciate me.

We began dating, and though their relationship had domestic issues, I became the provider and protector for her. We had a lot of differences in terms of culture, education, and background, but we made it work for a few years. In hindsight, I had a "what's love got to do with it?" mentality regarding my relationships. The attraction and fondness were there, but being "in love," probably not so much. I wanted to improve her quality of life, which was a consistent component of all my relationships. Perhaps it stems from my childhood, watching my mother after divorcing my father, and then her marrying my stepfather - how he treated us, protected us, and guided me as best he could until I left Iran. Security and stability are incredibly important aspects of a child's upbringing, and I did my best to provide that for my new wife's kids.

In the Middle Eastern culture, men are always responsible for providing for the house and family. Even in today's society, when women work and contribute financially, it's considered a "bonus" to the household finances and not expected. In many cultures, a man's leadership over the household is a combination of financial provisions, spiritual leadership, physical protection, preserving the family's reputation, and being able to serve his extended family as well. To serve God is to serve humanity, and that starts with his immediate family.

Like the Christians who believe that the husband should love his wife as Christ loved the church, the husband in Middle Eastern families puts the wants and needs of his wife above his own and even his children. Now, there's the age-old argument of whether we should put our children above ourselves in a selfless manner versus putting our spouse ahead of our children. Many people believe you should put God above all, then your spouse, then your children, and lastly yourself. Judaism, Islam, and Christianity are similar in terms of the care and provisions for the way they approach the responsibilities and roles within a family. Now, some lazy ass men call themselves "househusbands" and sit around watching porn and picking their noses all day. Some of these so-called men know how to make babies but don't stick around to raise them or even pay child support. Others will spend a fortune on their trucks, rifles, and other toys but complain about how their wife spends money on groceries or getting a pedicure every six months. Don't get me wrong – there are fools within both genders, but this area has never made sense regarding how we've "progressed" as a country.

I attended church out of respect for my then-wife and stepchildren and my church-leading in-laws. I was the leader of my home. I married a woman with children. I accepted those responsibilities, whereas I see men today want the "baby mama" but not the babies that come along with the package. I took my role seriously as I do everything I take on, and everybody involved, in turn, handles it better too.

On the career front, during that time, I was aiming for the Texas Highway Patrol, and in the words of Joe Pesci in "My Cousin Vinny," six times was the charm for me when I was finally accepted, not because I was a dumbass, but because there were over 20,000 applicants for just a few spots and we had to earn our spot for sure. I was number eight out of 9,000 to go to the academy. I was pushing hard in my career and set my mind on this goal, and I wanted it. Nothing was stopping me until I had an ACL rupture during training. I was so discouraged and I resigned to complete my physical therapy. I had been commuting between the Academy and Herne, Texas, so when I got back, I decided to visit family in the Washington D.C. area for a couple of weeks.

I returned a couple of days early from my trip and came home to a surprise. Let's just say the mouse has time to play when the cat's away, and that was the end of my first marriage. I took the high road for the kids' sake and my own. I'm not one to allow things to get muddled with emotions, and I took the practical route of ending our marriage. We had been married for five years by then, and that's when jher ex-husband called me personally to express his appreciation for making sure the kids didn't feel the backlash of the marriage ending. After everything was finalized with the divorce, I began a transition to East Texas and a renewed focus on my career.

You know, there's a reason why men from other countries

view American women in a stereotypical way. They are often thought of as "just for fun," whereas they'll marry a woman from their own country because they are typically more modest, loyal, family-oriented, and devoted to their husband and home. In Western cultures, women often need more attention and validation, especially when the man of the house is working, traveling, or occupied mentally with some other task for a given length of time. These are generalizations, of course, but stereotypes come from truth, and in my experience, it holds very true. People make mistakes, and I'm no saint, but I've maintained friendships with my exes despite our circumstances. Even after twenty years, I can say we communicate just fine, and she's raised two great kids.

Chapter 14
You're FIRED!

After my divorce, I began a new job in East Texas. The highway went straight from the Border through my new territory. I had scored first place on the agency's hiring tests, and I was hyped about US 59 running straight through where I could focus on interdiction and finally put my training to use. I had been learning and diving deeper into my continuing education for years, so I was pumped to get out on the highway and gain some real experience.

The first year was a probationary period of six months to one year. On my first stop, I seized 2 kilograms of cocaine. I was constantly learning, getting more loads, and looking for ways to further my career. To say that I was driven was an understatement. I was in a new city, in a new job, and soaking up every learning experience. I was asking questions, and my natural curiosity helped me to move through my days on the job with a healthy outlook and positive experiences. I came across people from all different backgrounds, religious affiliations, and stories. As the people I worked with learned about my own background, I quickly became the go-to resource when they had a stop with an individual of Middle Eastern descent. I'd get calls asking about the latest news headlines or my personal opinions on potential terrorist activities that we would hear about in the media. There were lots of questions based on misinformation in the media as well, and assumptions about individuals that fellow officers would stop while on duty.

I was working through my probation period about five months in when I got a call about a boyfriend who was threatening to come into town and kill his girlfriend. When I arrived, she got him on the phone, and I spoke to him in an attempt to set him straight and deter him from making a majorly wrong move. He said she "fucked up," and she had bought her a ticket to hell. Sounds like a nice guy, right? He lived seventy miles away but was threatening to come into town to teach her a lesson. She wanted me to sit on her house and watch it, which was obviously impossible. I wasn't in the private security business; I had a district to protect. So, when I spoke to him, I said, "I don't know why you say she fucked up when you're the one who fucked up because now you're going to have a record if you show up here." I prevented him from coming into town, but he ended up calling my department and filing a complaint against me, saying I used profanity. At the time, we had a new police chief who had started a couple of months before I did, and he wasn't too fond of me. I was still on new hire probation, but instead of recognizing the complaint for what it was, he used it as reason to dismiss me from duty for "violating policy" because I simply repeated the guy's language back to him on the call. Luckily, I had made friends in the next town over at the sheriff's office. Three weeks later, I was contacted by one of my coworkers, letting me know that he had a recording of the chief asking him if he knew where Pardazi was, and he told the chief that I had moved to the next county over. The chief told him, "If I had anything to do with it, his kind of people wouldn't be running around OUR country with a gun strapped to their belt." That was a conversation he had recorded on his agency's in-car camera by accident since he had just left the jail and was still recording the process as he ran across the chief in the hallway.

Now, those of you reading this in law enforcement are maybe thinking, "Boy, did I have a lawsuit on my hands," but I was so focused on my career and not becoming distracted that I didn't have a litigious mindset. The "blue brothers" mentality was overshadowed by the xenophobic reaction that I was exposed to; however, I knew that this was just a small percentage of law enforcement and didn't represent the majority of the diversity across all agencies. Could I have sued and been sitting fat and rich in a big house somewhere? Sure, but I was driven to excel in my career, and focusing on that was more important than getting a ticket for an easy way out. You can be blackballed and never work again if you do that, and my purpose was bigger than all that. I was focused on my career, not the projections of others. This wouldn't be the only time this kind of thing would happen to me, but I'll explain more about that later.

At that time, there was an increased amount of prejudice against anyone of Middle Eastern descent, mostly based on incorrect information and stereotypes. The war in Iraq was ongoing, there was always something negative and new about the Middle East. There were lots of casualties in Afghanistan as well, with American soldiers deployed all over the region. They took down Saddam Hussain and continued working on eliminating terrorist cells from different countries. In the US, Southeast Asian Indians were being attacked or assaulted when they were actually Sikhs and not Muslim. Men driving taxis or working in a store were insulted when they were Hispanic or another non-Middle Eastern nationality. People raised alarms at the sound of any foreign language being spoken, and everybody was on the lookout for any "suspicious activity" while out in public. This was when the "See Something, Say Something" campaign became widespread and average citizens were on high alert. I found myself on the answering end of many conversations during that time, educating friends and colleagues as much as I could.

One time, a few months after 9/11, when the debris and Ground Zero were still being processed and cleaned, I had a stop in the middle of the night while on the job. It was around 2 AM, out on a desolate stretch of highway in the middle of nowhere, in Deep East Texas. I stopped the vehicle for speeding. It was a rental van with Michigan plates. There were only two deputies working the whole county, and they were over thirty miles away from the stop. As law enforcement officers, we never know when a simple traffic stop can turn into something more, so backup is always an immediate consideration. The night was eerily quiet and still - you couldn't even hear the wildlife in the trees. Not a soul drove by, but I did what I always do – I walked up to the passenger side to introduce myself. I noticed four occupants in the vehicle with determined looks on their faces. I knew the look. They were all Arabs and had that look on their face that I had seen before when I was a kid being trained by Hezbollah.

The death stare they had on their face reminded me of the command staff of the guards in Iran, staring at all of us when we would get off the bus and get into formation for military training. The same look many of you have seen portrayed by the extremists who upload videos on social media to create fear in the minds of those who watch. I just knew deep down I'm up against some seriously dangerous folks. Imagine standing there in the middle of nowhere, not one soul around to help, and thinking, "Damn it, I've stopped some Al-Qaeda operatives, and they're going somewhere to blow something up, and here I am about to get blown up in the process." My mind was going a thousand miles per hour, but I also had to keep my composure and not show that I was fearful of what could happen. The last thing I needed is showing that I was literally shivering in my boots. I mean, who the hell wants to stop a car for speeding and then get caught up in a suicide bomber's last act?

Think about it, at the time, there was a considerable anger and hatred among mullahs and soldiers towards Americans, and these folks didn't know my nationality with it being dark outside, with only the moon and some light from my vehicle shining in our direction. My accent was not helping them with regard to my ethnicity either, and sometimes that works in my favor. The men were all dressed in *habayahs,* which is Arab attire, like a *thobe,* with *kufi* skull caps on their heads. Their beards were all the same; untrimmed, wild, and wiry, with no mustache.

Around that time, I had been watching the news where they reported insurgents killing American soldiers simply because they represented Western culture. I didn't think I was any different; I was a representative of the country's police force. They wouldn't see me as a Middle Eastern cop, and they were very apprehensive about identifying themselves. Two of the men had Michigan licenses, and the other two had only Canadian passports. I asked the driver to exit the vehicle so that I could issue the citation. During my conversation with him, I noticed that he was extremely deceptive as he explained that they were on the way to meet some colleagues at a mosque in Houston, Texas. In my mind, I was thinking that as a Muslim, he would be happy and excited to share his activities and plans, but he wasn't. His behavior was very concerning, to say the least.

I had him stand on the side of the road while I went to my car and ran his license and the names of the other passengers through our dispatch. While sitting in my car, watching the driver and the car to make sure none of them jumped out and began an assault, waiting on dispatch to come over the radio and give me an all-clear, I grabbed my M-4 Rifle and placed it on my lap. That's right, I wasn't taking any chances. If they would have decided to get into a gunfight, we were having it, and I was going to send them to get their so-called 72 virgins. Luckily, none made any moves while I was sitting in my car.

About a minute or so later, the radio beeped and dispatch called my number, followed by a silence. I heard the voice of the dispatcher crack in the process. I knew something was worrying her. I grabbed the radio mic and answered. She came back on and, still with a shaky voice, asked for my exact location. Now I'm definitely getting worried. This is not usual for a dispatcher to want my exact location down to the next cross street. Mind you, I know that the other two deputies are well over thirty minutes from my location. So the hair on the back of my neck is now at full attention and standing straight up. I felt that tingling in my ears, and I could feel my blood pressure skyrocketing. In a matter of three seconds, I thought about so many things. Things like, "Shit, they're wanted, and I'll have to try to arrest these bastards all by myself with only two handcuffs and no back up." Then thinking: "And what if they attack me?" and so many other scenarios. It was one of those situations that had me going through a roller coaster of "What ifs."

Now, don't get me wrong. I knew if I had to take care of business, it was going to be taken care of for sure. At that time in my career, I was in the best shape too. I ran five miles a day before work and spent two hours at the gym lifting heavy weights. I was rock solid. To the point that I wore an extra large bulletproof vest. But, because I was short, they had to cut it into an extra small torso size. I benched 460 pounds at the time. And for a dude who only weighed 182 pounds, that was a monster of a weight. I was bulky and walked around like I had two large watermelons under my arms. Not because I wanted to, but those lat muscles poked out way past my underarms.

As I answered the dispatcher and told her my exact location (between Nacogdoches and Lufkin, Texas), she asked if my radio was "secure." This is usually done in preparation for revealing information that could be related to officer safety, and they don't want the suspect to hear it. Of course, I was in my car, and the dude standing outside couldn't hear me, so I told her to go ahead and speak.

She opened the mic and told me to use extreme caution and continued to tell me that two of the four are listed on the Terror Watch List by the FBI as Priority One Entries. I knew exactly what that meant. That meant these dudes weren't some jack-asses who may have been on the FBI's radar and were just being watched; they were the real deal, meaning they had to be taken into custody. I had no clue if there were any bombs or weapons in the vehicle or on them personally.

I used my radio to call for the other deputies and local police to make their way to my location. I exited the car with my rifle at my shoulder and ordered the driver to the ground, and stood above him with my rifle pointed straight toward the van. I ordered all the rest to raise their hands outside the windows and not make a move, or I would shoot them all at once. I know it sounds harsh, but I'd rather take them out before they decide to blow themselves up and take me with them.

I held that position for about eighteen minutes, not making any more sounds, and neither did they. They kept their hands extended outside of each window next to them. That eighteen minutes felt like five hours. I could hear the sirens coming from miles away. And man, I can tell you it was the best feeling in the world. I mean, the entire time we were out there, only six cars had passed us. It was literally dead out there. If I would have been shot, I would have probably not been found until sunrise, so I wasn't taking any chances.

After the cavalry arrived, we tactically removed all the passengers and secured them. There were so many documents in the car, along with six huge suitcases filled with papers, clothes, and all kinds of written materials, as well as about sixty cellular phones. As the other officers watched the suspects in their cars, I quickly looked through some of the larger items in the van to make sure we weren't standing next to bomb-making material or any weapons. Once I was able to determine that no immediate threat was present, I closed off the car and called for a wrecker.

The communications center told me over the radio that the FBI was headed to our county from Houston (almost a three-hour drive), and they requested that the subjects be taken to the office and held until they arrive. So, we did just that.

But about two hours later, six FBI agents arrived. They must have been driving over 100 MPH to get there. This indicated to me these dudes were pretty high up in the food chain for the FBI to get out of bed after midnight and haul ass to such a desolate location. How do I know this? It's very well known that unless someone or something is that important, the FBI usually doesn't come to any location and requests only the information and reports to be forwarded to them. But, for them to play Johnny on the spot, it's something extremely important.

The agents spent about fifteen minutes at the office coordinating and hopped back in their cars, with each car taking two of the suspects. One agent jumped in the van, and they were gone from our office within thirty minutes of arriving. All I was told is to make sure none of the names were released or placed in any reports. I was happy because I didn't even have to do a report. What a great catch for me. All the excitement of catching some terrorists and no paperwork? Hell yeah, I'll do that again!

Needless to say, it would not be the first or last time I've partaken in similar stops. Many stops within my career on the road resulted in the identification and apprehension of potential threats to national security. These types of cases are not open to the public like others you may hear about in the local or national news due to them being national security-related investigations. This is the reason you may hear the FBI say terms like "We cannot confirm nor deny....." That pretty much means freedom of the press doesn't extend to those investigations, and rightfully so. Imagine being at the brink of taking down a terror cell plotting to blow up a building with civilians inside somewhere in the country, and some reporter trying to make a name reveals the operation. Sometimes the public is better off not knowing certain things because it could and will cost more lives.

I spent the next two years on a statewide task force working all over the State of Texas, identifying and capturing smugglers. And being a Middle Easterner, I was also summoned to assist with a wide array of other investigations that required my overseas knowledge and skillset. But, as you can tell by now, those are matters of national security, and nope, I ain't going to prison for publishing details about them. Let's just say there are some really bad people in the world, and some of the things that happen need to stay secret.

After two years, state funding grants for our task force ended. I was faced with another transition in my career. My faith, my ambitions, and my goals propelled me forward yet again. I had an opportunity to move to Mississippi, so another move in the Deep South was on the horizon. As a single guy living in a rental home, it was an easy decision. I was ready for another move. And boy, was it an adventure full of ups and downs.

Chapter 15
The Move It Is

I decided to move to Mississippi to further my career in the field of transnational smuggling and counter-terrorism investigations and began working in a specialized unit in May 2005. This was the peak of my law enforcement career in national security after 9/11. I began working with various local, state, and federal agencies on their anti-terrorism/anti-smuggling training, and my phone was ringing around the clock from friends and colleagues. I was the resource for understanding the various Middle Eastern factions and terrorist groups. Each extremist group has different motives and purposes for their actions, with variables that determined how they would move around the world. For law enforcement and intelligence agencies to combat this new threat, simply learning to translate a language was not enough to identify and foil any plots against the homeland and on US assets abroad. They needed to understand why these groups were committing these acts of terrorism and the deep-rooted mentality behind it all.

Even though many in the law enforcement and intelligence community were in contact with me on a regular basis, asking about Middle Eastern-related topics, no one really asked me about my religion. I assume because I had been previously married to Christians, the fact that I was a cop, and while I interacted with and worked with people of different backgrounds, religion didn't come up as cultural details did. They must have simply assumed I was a Christian. It's pretty common to assume Muslims don't believe in Jesus, but the reality is that one can't be a Muslim and *not* believe in Jesus Christ. There is an entire chapter in the Quran dedicated to the Virgin Mary and the Virgin Birth of Jesus Christ as the Messiah. An educated Muslim also knows that at the end of the time, according to Islamic teachings, Jesus will return to fight the Antichrist. Now, you read this as a Westerner and think: "What? I didn't know that!" It's true. You can simply Google it. But I would also be very careful what you Google; remember when I mentioned about Hadith and interpretations and how it gets corrupted. In today's world and with the ease of use of the internet and websites, anyone can throw up a PHP website, buy a domain from GoDaddy, and create an official-looking website while spreading misinformation, and there are millions of them out there. All I can suggest is to know the validity of the source. Also, keep in mind, as a Muslim, I am in no position to explain the details about Christianity or Judaism, meaning my opinions would be conjecture and not facts. When learning about a specific religion, the best source is to be objective and ensure those who are speaking of the religion are either from the academic background with PhDs in the field or scholars and theologians from that specific religion. I don't take interpretations from some street preacher who just got out of the penitentiary. Just like evidence that has to be verified, the information sought must be verified and validated that it's coming from a legitimate source.

During the time mentioned, I became the "unofficial expert," set apart from other law enforcement officers from other areas of the country. My professional network was growing, and I had more opportunities to work on transnational smuggling "narco-terrorism" projects. The CIA, Mossad, and other intelligence agencies around the world all require agents to have additional cultural and religious expertise and training. Some even finance higher education for their operatives to obtain PhDs in the fields and live abroad to learn the culture. Translating a note isn't enough to stop the masterminds behind the biggest terrorist groups around the world. These individuals are raised by generational conditioning since birth, and this requires federal and international law enforcement and intelligence agency attention at the deepest level. A prime example of how intelligence communities around the world embedded themselves in these realms is the story of Eli Cohen, an Egyptian-born Israeli Jew who grew up speaking Arabic and went on to be a Mossad operative, penetrating the ranks of the Syrian government in the 1960s. He is hailed as a hero for Israel, and rightfully so. He would not have been able to do such an operation if he didn't have in-depth knowledge of the culture and religious practices. Even though he was a Jew, he spoke Arabic and attended prayers at the mosques. Would you, as the reader, be able to go to a Mosque and interact with the congregation and actually partake in the daily ritual prayers? I assume not unless you're in the intelligence community in a non-official cover status. It would be impossible to do such an act and not be identified. You'd need years and years of complex training and in-depth knowledge of the traditions, culture, and religious practices. You can see why during the time in America when Al-Qaeda posed the biggest threat, someone like me would be the source where most local, state, and federal agencies would turn to for assistance.

Being in law enforcement and already having associates at all levels, plus being Middle Easterner, yet opened more opportunities for me. When I was living in Texas, I was approached by the FBI to work on Homeland Security issues in addition to specialized positions for Counter-Smuggling. As a sworn federal task force agent, I was summoned to assist in working on national security cases, terrorism surveillance, identifying and recruiting assets stateside and abroad, and translating documents. Due to the nature of these cases, specific cases cannot be shared, as any investigation regarding national security will never be made public. They called it Top Secret for a reason. And trust me, I'm not one who wants to be locked up for life at Leavenworth Prison. I escaped the Middle East to enjoy Life, Liberty, and the Pursuit of Happiness. How is that even possible in a 6X9 cell?

As I continued my career, my focus was split in three directions: First, my personal struggles "Jihad," which was to excel, educate, and combat the challenges that came my way; Second, to help the USA and the agencies that are tasked with protecting the citizens; and Third, my goals for my career and family.

What is "Jihad" ?

Jihad (n.) is a word in Islam that means a struggle or fight against the enemies of Islam; it can also mean the spiritual struggle within oneself against sin.

During this time, there were a lot of misunderstandings and racial confusion around the world. Among certain groups, we could joke about the confusion without animosity or real threat.

For example, among Iranians in the United States, it was common for non-Iranians to ask if we spoke Arabic (Iranians typically speak a regional dialect of Farsi, and in some areas, they may also speak Turkish, Kurdish, or Armenian) or if we were "Arabic" (as in, nationality). At times when local folks in the deep south found out that I was Muslim, I would observe a change in their demeanor, and what was once warm and friendly communication would turn cold and reserved. So, I kept my interactions to a minimum and with friends and colleagues that knew me well. My focus was to continue to excel in my career.

One day, I was at the bank drive-thru with a friend of mine, and we both noticed an attractive teller in the bank window. A few days later, I began asking about her from the locals I knew and found out that she had been doing the same. It's common to be a creature of habit in the South, so it didn't take long for us to connect. She was a divorced Christian Palestinian woman with a young son. Now, you may be thinking that with my religious upbringing and cultural mentality, how would I come to date yet another Christian woman?

Marrying Christian women wasn't a problem for me or even my extended family. In some relationships, the religion is so strong, it becomes a cultural identity and therefore, there can be some "culture shock" when the couple marries and learns to navigate relationships with extended family, holidays, and how to raise the children. For me, it was simply a matter of communication, mutual respect, and coming to an agreement on the issues of religion, kids, and so on.

Well, I understood her situation, and our morals and cultural values were similar, or at the very least, understandable. She had come to the United States for an arranged marriage (Yes, the Middle Eastern Christians do that too), and when she learned he wasn't what he claimed, she sought a divorce. We had a great relationship, but because of cultural traditions and her family being concerned for her reputation and well-being, we decided to get married. Remember, dating is not allowed in the Middle East. It comes with a lot of negative assumptions that are reflected to an entire family or tribe. We were content for a while until she made a new Christian Syrian friend who had some brothers overseas that needed a way to come to the US. This new friend manipulated my then-wife and persuaded her over time that one brother, in particular, would be a better match for her than the Iranian Muslim she had married.

Her mother was visiting with us at the time and learned of the friend's master plan and expressed her concern to her daughter. Not only did she not heed her mother's warning, she put her on a plane back to the homeland and then asked me for a divorce. I took the same approach as the first marriage, wanting her child to be cared for and to end the marriage amicably. I knew she had been brainwashed by her friend, but the damage had already been done. She wanted out, and I obliged her. Years later, she realized her mistake, but at that point, we had both moved on.

I had to decide if I wanted to move again, and being in a diverse area in Texas has always appealed to me. Remember, I loved to eat, and there were Middle Eastern markets and restaurants in Texas and none in Mississippi! Friends and colleagues were always in my ear, trying to persuade me to move here or there. I was at another pivotal point in my life and was headed toward another major life change.

After the divorce, I focused on my work and dated here and there, but nothing significant happened for a while. Then I met Lilly. It was a whirlwind relationship, we got married, and nine months later, my son Kamran was born. Lilly already had a son and daughter, so we began our marriage with a full house and life as a new father for the first time in my life to my own flesh-and-blood "Seyed." My little Kamran became my reason for living and my focus for everything, including my career. It wasn't enough to commit to goals for myself anymore. I had a family that depended on me, I was happily married, and life was good. We would go on family trips to take Lilly to meet my extended family, and she began learning about Iranian culture and even Islam. I didn't know it at the time, but Lilly decided she wanted to learn about Islam to teach Kamran, and even she surprised me when she completed her conversion. We had many friends and acquaintances in Mississippi by then, and when her family learned of her conversion, it created a lot of detachment and resentment towards our family.

On Saturday, March 17th, 2018, around 10:00 AM, I was awakened by a panicking wife. I had been at work the night before, arriving home at 4:00 AM. When I opened my eyes, I saw Lilly's face white as a ghost. Her lips were almost bluish-purple, and she was rapidly taking shallow breaths. I sprang up and asked her what was going on. She couldn't talk much between the breaths and was able to force out the words "I can't breathe." I didn't know what to do. I'm not an EMT, and other than knowing how to put on a band-aid, I didn't know much else. She mumbled she was going to the emergency room and she had called her Yemeni friend "Ella" to come and take her since I had to stay home and watch the kids.

The kids, who were six, three, and two, were still in bed. We kept late nights on the weekend since I worked nights. Lilly would stay up for me to get home, so we could eat and go to bed together, which was our nightly routine. As I rolled out of bed and started to get ready for the day, Ena arrived. She walked in, and she and I helped Lilly get into her car. Lilly, who was weak and could barely speak, looked at me, gave me a kiss, and said, "I love you!" I never thought that would be her last words to me. They left, and I started to make breakfast, hoping to wake up the kids. I knew I'd have to go to the hospital and potentially take the kids if I couldn't get someone to watch them.

It had been about thirty minutes since they left for the hospital when I was in the kitchen, trying to make coffee and get some breakfast ready. My phone rang and it was Lilly's number, but when I answered, I heard Ena's voice. Crackling and in a high pitch, she said, "You have to get here NOW!" I asked her, "What happened?" It was so scary because I had no clue what had happened. They weren't even gone thirty minutes yet. Ena, who seemed like she was tearing up, said to me, "Shawn, they took her and admitted her immediately to the Critical Care Unit." I froze in place. I didn't know what to think. I feel a chill go down my spine. I got goosebumps, and my head started to feel the pressure as my blood started rushing to my head. My heart rate was now elevated, and I could hear my heartbeat in my ears and the sound of the blood rushing into my skull. As I started to ask her, "What the hell....." she interrupted me and said she went unconscious, and they think she has severe pneumonia.

There I was, standing in the kitchen, holding an empty coffee mug in my hand, immediately thinking to myself, "How the hell am I supposed to go with three kids here by themselves?" I started to panic, and before I could get another word out, I heard Ena say, "I'm leaving to come get the kids, get ready, and be out the door as I drive up." I turned the coffee pot off, and in the midst of the chaos in my head, I didn't even realize I had dropped the coffee cup on the kitchen floor and it had shattered. The porcelain cup was in pieces all over the floor. I never even noticed dropping it. Never heard the sound. I was in another realm of consciousness. I ran into the bedroom, grabbed the first pair of jogging pants I could find, the first shirt in my t-shirt drawer, and threw on my tennis shoes. I quickly brushed my teeth, grabbed my gym bag, and headed to my car. My patrol car, a blacked-out Tahoe, was in the garage. I didn't care that I wasn't in uniform. My wife was being admitted to the CCU, and I wasn't worried about the consequences. I just wanted to get there, but I couldn't just leave. The kids were still in bed, having no clue as to what was happening, and I couldn't leave them. All I could think of was how long before Ena gets here.

I opened the garage door, cranked my car, and paced back and forth in the driveway, waiting for Ena's SUV to come into my sight. What seemed like an hour later, when it was literally about three minutes after I had opened the garage door, I saw her maroon SUV top the hill and rapidly approach our house. As she screeched into the driveway, she exited wearing her hijab and had a look on her face that screamed, "I'm panicking." That didn't help me much. I was hoping I would calm down when she showed up, expecting her to tell me it was going to be okay. But that wasn't the case. She yelled at me, "Go, go, go, Yala, I will get the kids."

As she barged through the garage area, opening the door into the kitchen, I saw Kamran through the door. I hear him say, "Momma." She grabbed him and shut the door behind her. By this time, I was in the front seat of my police Tahoe and rolling backward down our steep driveway. I sped out of the driveway, lights, and siren. I didn't care how fast I was going. I had to be there NOW. The ER was about two and a half miles from my house. But there were three red lights and two stop signs, and I had to drive down three different streets to get there. The traffic was usually bad because of the businesses in the area, but since it was Saturday, I expected less traffic. As I entered the main road, Highway 493, I kicked it into high gear. I must have driven well over 100 MPH for the first mile. As I drove to the hospital, all I could think of was, "What happened? What made her so ill? What's going to happen?" There were so many other questions rolling through my head, I don't even remember the whole trip. All I remember is I screeched into the ambulance bay at the ER, parked my car, left the lights going, and ran into the ER.

I didn't know any of the staff since I didn't deal with medical issues on the job and had never been to the only ER in town. My job was to work in desolate areas of the state on rural interstate highways, catching terrorists and smugglers. There was no need for me to mingle or visit the medical facilities like most cops do when they deal with normal police calls. Somehow, they all knew who I was and what I was doing there. The security guy at the entrance just pointed to the right of the ER nurses' station to a set of double doors. One nurse said, "CCU is through the door and to the right, GO!" I ran through the hallways of the ER, thinking, "how do they know why I'm here, I don't know these people," but that thought was gone in an instant. As I blasted through the double doors, I saw another set of double doors on my right and a nurse standing there, holding the automatic doors open. She must have been told by the ER people that I was on the way and held the one-way opening door open for me to go straight into the CCU.

I ran into the main floor of the CCU and immediately noticed room 128 is packed with about nine medical staff. I saw Lilly's face, and she seemed lethargic. I came into the room slowly, and one of the medical staff said, "Stay there for a second, let us get her machines hooked up first." I froze in place, standing less than four feet from my wife, who was now breathing shallow breaths and was pale white. Her lips were literally the color purple. I had never seen her like that, but I have seen that complexion before, and I knew she was lacking oxygen. I looked at the monitor and saw her SATs are at 78 percent. I'm by no means knowledgeable in medical statuses, but I knew that SAT levels being that low was NOT GOOD AT ALL.

About a minute had passed and I was just standing there, out of the way in room 128 of the CCU at Anderson Hospital in Meridian, Mississippi. I knew this was not a Level 1 or 2 trauma center and was worried. As a man, I saw my wife in a position that made me want to get the best help for her and immediately. But I also knew there were limitations each facility has. The male nurse, who had hooked up an IV to her, told me, "Hey, come tell her you're here because we have to sedate her and intubate her. She's suffering from a really bad infection in her lungs, and we have to relax her." He rolled his roller chair out of the way, and I walked up and held Lilly's hand. She had a mask over her head, and she was breathing so fast it sounded like she had just ran 1000 yards at a full sprint. I lowered my head and said in her ear, "Hey babe, I'm here. I love you!" She barely opened her eyes, looked at me, and blinked with both eyes. She was then out of consciousness. That was the last time I saw her eyes open, her sky-blue eyes radiating towards me. I didn't know what to say. I stepped back, and the nurses went back to work. They kicked me out of the room and escorted me to the waiting area.

As soon as I got there, the hospital security showed up, most of whom were retired cops, and asked if I needed anything. I couldn't even talk. One of them grabbed me and said, 'We got you, brother. We'll be here if you need us." I then remembered my patrol car was still in the ambulance bay and was taking up one of the spaces. I asked one of the security guys if he could move it and secure it somewhere. He took the keys to take care of it.

As I sat down, a million questions were going through my head. So many "what if's" I didn't have an answer for. The concern of wanting to know what would happen. As a man who plans and has to have all the scenarios answered, not knowing what would happen is the most stressful position. It can drive one nuts. I started to text her family. I texted her younger sister Hannah, who was in town and married at the time, the little details I had. She agreed to notify the rest of the family, and I started calling my own family back in Arizona and Alabama. I texted one of my co-workers to let him know I would be taking off. What was funny is that it didn't seem like it was a big deal to him. Turns out, he was the biggest piece of trash I had ever met. He was one of the same guys who, just two months after Lilly's passing, would call me and tell me I needed to hurry up and get back to work. I'll just leave it at that for you to figure out the empathy this dude had for people.

I waited for a couple of hours in the waiting room, then one of the nurses came out of the CCU to tell me I can go in for a quick visit. The CCU had set visitation hours and would limit the number of visitors since every patient was closely monitored. Having too many people in the CCU at various times would obviously make it difficult to deal with emergencies for the staff. What I found kind was that since the staff had been told I was in law enforcement and a lot of nurses were either married to cops or were family to cops, they decided to move her from room 128 to 129, which was at the end of the CCU floor, near the side entrance at the end of the hallway that was open to the public. Apparently, the head CCU nurse and manager had decided to bypass the strict visitation schedule for me by placing her near the end, close to an exit door, so I could sneak in and out without being noticed by others.

That day, into the night, I visited with her intermittently. I spent a lot of time in the waiting room, answering texts, calls and updating those who had been messaging me. In a matter of eight hours, I had over 2000 messages on social media since the news had been spread throughout the world. I was getting messages from friends, family, and folks I know all the way from Jordan, Iraq, Switzerland, the UK, New Zealand, and Venezuela.

There was no way for me to stay on social media, so I decided to do several public updates on Facebook as the day went on. The posts were being shared, and the sheer number of support and kind words were helping me cope with the unknowns. The medical staff was conducting hundreds of tests that day to try to determine what had gone wrong and decide what treatment options had to be implemented.

It was the weekend, and a lot of the specialists weren't available to come, but efforts were being made by summoning phone advice from doctors all the way from California and New York. I wasn't involved in that at all, but every time I would sneak into the CCU with their permission, one of the nurses would update me with the latest information. As the night fell, I was drained. I hadn't eaten at all. I couldn't eat. I felt weak and worried not only for Lilly but also for the kids. I knew the kids were in good hands for the time being, but at the same time wondered what they were being told and what was going through their minds. I couldn't help but think if she doesn't recover, what would have been the last thing the kids remember about Lilly since they had seen her before they went to bed and woke up to her being gone to the hospital. The sheer number of questions rummaging through my head was astonishing, and I had no answers. It just added more and more to the anxiety I felt.

It was after midnight when Lilly's older sister arrived with her kids. They stopped at the hospital to get the keys to my house and went to leave their stuff. She came back to the hospital around 2 AM to stay with me and check on updates. She hadn't seen Lilly yet. We were able to sneak into the CCU around 3 AM to see Lilly. Lilly was now hooked up to about eighteen lines of different medications, and there were machines everywhere. The life support machine was to the right of the bed, numerous IV lines were hanging on two separate racks to the left of her bed, and a few other machines were at the foot of her bed. She was just lying there, motionless, under sedation.

We spent about twenty minutes talking to her, but she was unconscious. We were hoping she could at least hear us.

The sound of the life support machine popping, as the balloon would go up and down, was a scary sound. All I could think of was, "what if the electricity goes out, what happens then?" The other thoughts were still there. I felt like a helpless person, at the mercy of God and what the medical staff could do, and had no power nor idea of what I could do. I wanted answers, and there weren't any. There were two nurses assigned to her room. They had to be always present. Which I was told was not a normal thing. One nurse told me that two additional nurses were called in just to be assigned to her, so the other six nurses could take care of the other 22 patients that occupied the CCU floor.

Once we finished the visit, we went back to the waiting area, which was empty overnight. I decided I needed to lay my head down and get some sleep. Drained beyond belief and feeling like I had been run over physically by a Mack truck, I placed three chairs next to each other and commandeered a blanket from the nurse's station. It was around 5 AM when I finally closed my eyes. I must have fallen asleep so fast and deep because I don't remember anything other than pulling the covers over my head to block the solid white LED lights from shining on my face.

All of a sudden, I'm awakened by a loud beep and a female's voice saying, "Code Blue 129, Code Blue 129." I opened my eyes, hearing a lot of commotion. I looked over at Tamra, Lilly's older sister, and she said, "Wait, what is that? Isn't that her room number?" As soon as she utters those words, we see over ten nurses running down the hallway from various directions and all headed to the CCU main entrance door. They all barge in the door, and the door automatically closes behind them. This is one of those double doors that have no handles, and one would have to have a card to open. Access to the interior was restricted. I get up and walk to the door, trying to peek in the crack to see what is going on in the CCU. The door is not facing Lilly's room since her room was at the end of the hallway to the right. As I'm standing there, three other medical staff are now coming to the same door, and I can tell from their lab coats that they are medical doctors. They push me aside and tell me to go back to the waiting area. They didn't know who I was. I assume they thought I was some stranger just being nosey.

This is all happening in about a one-minute period. I'm so curious as to what is "Code Blue," when the door opened and they barged in, I asked a young lady, who I later found out was a CNA, "What is Code Blue?" She said, "Sir, you can't be in here, and that means it's a cardiac arrest." I immediately asked, "In room 129?" and she nodded, "Yes." I think she then realized that I was the husband. She walked over to me and started to tell me that "It'll be okay; let's go back to the waiting area. They're working on her, and it looks like they got her back." I was frozen. I couldn't move. I burst out crying like a little kid. I fell to my knees and started praying. I couldn't even say a word. I felt another person's hand on my shoulder and realized Tamra had now come to the door and had heard what she said. She helped me up, tears in her eyes, and started to pull me toward the waiting area. The CNA went back into the CCU, and Tamra and I walked back to the waiting area. I was so numb. I couldn't think. The only thing on my mind was, "Please, God, Please save her. It's not time. She has so much to live for. She's only 28." The thoughts of losing her, the kids, and many other potential outcomes were going through my head nonstop. Tamra, who was trying to deal with her own emotions and mine at the same time, was speaking to me, but I could not hear her. To this day, I can't remember anything she said.

For the next thirty minutes, I sat in a chair that gave me a clear view of the hallway, trying to see when these nurses would come out. They finally did and seemed relieved. I could tell because 25 years of specialized training in subconscious communication and human behavior has enabled me to read facial expressions and body language. As one of the nurses walked by, I recognized her. She was the nurse that was in the ER the day before. She also recognized me. She walked over and said, "She's safe for now. Very critical, but we got her back. Once they stabilize her more, they'll come and talk to you. Hang in there. They're doing all they can."

She walked off, and we sat there. I was crying, angry, confused, hungry, and at the same time, felt nauseous. I can't even explain the abundance of emotions and had never felt that type of complex emotional effect. It doesn't even compare to the fear I felt in Iran, thinking I would die if I didn't escape. Not many have experienced that in their lifetime. Most hear about a relative's death after it has happened. Here I was, in the midst of a potentially worst outcome and walking through it as a potential end result. All with no control or say so and no knowledge of what to expect. All I knew was I wanted to fix it, and I didn't know how, along with feeling scared, helpless, and confused all at the same time. All I knew to do was pray. I posted an update on social media as the day started. I didn't have time to respond or reply to folks. So, I didn't go back and read the comments until a couple of weeks later. As the day went on, other family members showed up. Friends drove in to show support, and some even ordered food and had it sent to the hospital for the family, who were all now camped out in the large waiting area.

A few hours later, things are back to normal, until around 1 PM, when the loudspeaker goes off with the words "Code Blue 129" and repeats twice. Within five hours of hearing the same words the first time, I heard it again. The same exact scenario plays out. Throughout the day, that announcement was broadcasted five times in a matter of thirteen hours. I was a wreck. I can't even begin to explain my feelings and thoughts now. I must have blocked it all. All I remember is the third time, the staff was using a LUCAS machine. The mechanical chest compression machine that I had seen on life flights that responded to accident scenes I had been on when someone was being flown to the nearest Level 1 Trauma center. Between the third and fourth coding, they allowed me and Tamra in the room for a short time. I noticed a tube coming out of the side of Lilly's chest. The nurse said that her rips had been broken and her lung had collapsed, so they had to put a tube in. I could see the yellow puss and blood dripping down the tube into a container. This was my wife. Just imagine seeing your loved one, lifeless, with all the machines and tubes hanging off her; a sight that is hardly describable. It was pure madness.

She didn't code anymore that day and stayed the same vitals for the next two days. The staff at the CCU were so warm and helpful. Except for the one issue we noticed. Tamra had brought an iPad and had it affixed to the headboard of the bed. She had the Quran Recitation playing in Arabic at a very low volume the entire time. It was so low that you'd have to kneel into the headboard of the bed to barely hear the recitation. Just standing there in the room, it was not noticeable. It wasn't there for everyone. It was for Lilly to hear. She had realized the staff was turning it off when we weren't in the room. According to a couple of nurses that worked the night shift, one of the older nurses who worked during the day kept turning it off and claimed they "didn't like hearing that *shit*" because they were Islamic prayers in Arabic. I guess there are bigots in every career field, and the medical field is no different. I just chucked it up to ignorance. We had other issues to be concerned about.

There were concerns that she wasn't passing any liquids. Wednesday night, an emergency dialysis was ordered around 2 AM. The machine couldn't help, and on Thursday morning, March 22, 2018, the specialist decided to do exploratory surgery to determine what was happening. She was too unstable, even for life flight and to do MRIs or CT scans. They started around

7:30 AM. I laid down on a chair in the waiting area again after taking a shower in an empty room, as one of the nurses was gracious enough to allow me to do so. I must have fallen asleep for about an hour when I felt a tap on my shoulder. I was alone in the waiting room. Tamra had left to go check on her kids, as she did several times a day. I woke up, and a nurse from the CCU told me that the doctor wanted to see me in the conference room. I was not quite awake, and when I looked at her face, I could see the sadness. I had a bad feeling about this encounter. She helps me up and hugs me. I can tell she's motioning to someone as she looks over my shoulder. Two other nurses were walking out of the CCU and came toward us. The original nurse asked me, "Where's your sister-in-law?" I told her she went to check on the kids. She tells me to call her and have her return.

Now I know what's going on. She's making sure I have someone near because I'm about to get bad news. The same type of arraignment that is usually made when a cop delivers a death notification. This is obvious. I tell the nurse, let's go. I'll be okay. It's been five days, and I'm prepared for the worst. She doesn't say a word. She just turns and steps aside, letting me lead the way to the main doors of the CCU. We get to the door, and she opens it, directing us to the left into a room with a small round table and four chairs. I sit there for about thirty seconds, and the doctor walks in. Still wearing his operating room scrubs and the operating room cap, he sits down, looks me dead in my eyes, and says, "I'm sorry, Shawn, we couldn't save her." I just looked at him and asked, "What did you find?" He said that they had opened her to see what was going on with her kidneys and realized that all her organs were already black. Which meant that she had been deceased for at least the last 72 hours, and the only thing keeping her body functioning was the meds. I dropped my head, started crying, and that's all I remember. The rest of the day was a blur.

My beautiful wife, Lilly, passed! *"Inna lillahi wa inna ilayhi reji'un"* (Verify we belong to Allah, and truly to Him shall we return.) You may be familiar with the phrase "dust to dust"; it's from the Book of Genesis in the Bible –*'we therefore commit this body to the ground, earth to earth, ashes to ashes, dust to dust you shall return.'* The concept of returning the body, whether cremated or buried, back to the Earth applies in many religions.

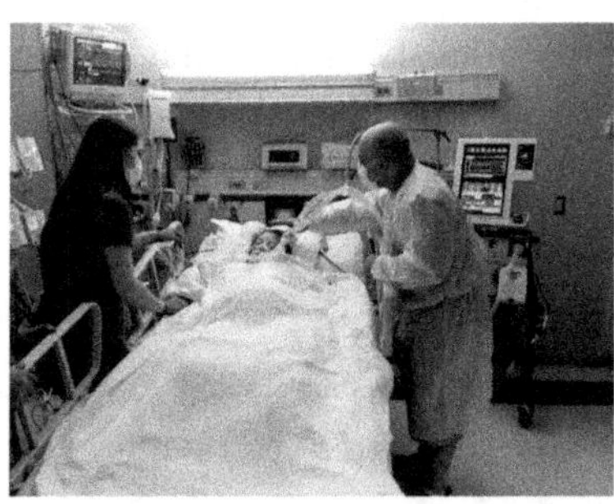

I felt like my world was shattered. My focus had to shift quickly to survival mode for Kamran and many who have followed my career. I had to go back to work, so close friends took care of Kamran while I bounced back and forth. During that time, I was waiting on Lilly's headstone to be completed. When it was installed, I began taking Kamran there to visit her grave. I had so many personal messages that I couldn't keep up with from family, friends, and colleagues all over the world that I figured the best and easiest way to update everyone was through social media posts. A few weeks into posting and sharing photos and summary updates, I noticed a change in the demeanor of the locals around me. My colleagues were excluding me from lunches or meet-ups. They would go silent when I needed backup. Now, this isn't something new in the law enforcement world. Anyone who's ever been "shunned" by their colleagues can relate. I started connecting the dots, and while it's not a great feeling to know you're no longer welcome where you work, for a law enforcement officer, it can be deadly when you aren't supported by the people who work with you and provide backup.

I experienced two years of chaos, working full time, teaching, and being a mom and dad while those I worked with continued to shun me. I learned not to depend on those who wouldn't show up as backup on a stop.

When her headstone was installed, it clearly showed the Islamic symbol on it. I had posted a lot of the pictures on social media, so the symbol was very apparent in the photos. It didn't take long before her grave started being sabotaged; thus, it made sense why the shunning had commenced. Kamran and I often went to the grave, and we started noticing that Kamran's toys were being broken to pieces. The flowers and lighting I had installed were destroyed over and over. When it comes to getting things done, I don't do anything on a small scale if I can help it, and Lilly's grave was no different. Needless to say, it's the most elaborate headstone in the entire cemetery, decorated with her smiling image, a huge slab, and solar lighting to make sure it's lit up all throughout the night. She was my wife and the mother of my child. I wanted to do everything I could to celebrate her life and give Kamran a way to visit his mother and keep her memory alive so her gravesite draws the most attention in the cemetery.

During those two years, I went through several nannies, caregivers as well as friends who filled the void and were a safe place for Kamran while I managed to keep going. My mom was in Iran, worried about us, and offered to find me a wife in Iran who could care for Kamran and finally be the Iranian wife she hoped would be the answer for me. I was not in the right frame of mind to look for a new relationship, and I sure wasn't in the mood to walk around a mall or something with my son and an imported woman that looked like a penguin in a black cloak in the middle of the deep South! I was already receiving derogatory and underhanded comments directly and on social media. Can you imagine already being looked at in a negative light and walking around the mall or eating at a restaurant with a woman in a full hijab? I know how that works; I've been there and seen it firsthand when I was eating at places, and a Muslim man would walk in with his wife and daughters wearing hijabs. The look on some of the people's faces was of contempt. I can't even recall how many times the underhanded comments were made by patrons referring to them as "terrorists" and "Sleeper Cells." I surely wasn't about to be looked at in the same light, especially knowing just about everyone in the community knew what I did for a living.

I continued to take Kamran to his mother's grave to have picnics so he could play and have memories of being there at different ages. He was a little boy, so how much do toddlers understand about losing a parent? I didn't want it to be uncomfortable for him or scary like it can be for some people as they grow older. That was his mother's resting place, and I wanted him to feel comfortable visiting and talking to her. Even to this day, there is camera surveillance equipment monitoring her grave. But when I moved from the area in June 2020, all negative activities ceased. Isn't that funny? It's almost as if the offending culprits just wanted to make me uncomfortable enough to leave town. If that was the case, I would have left as soon as it started, but I don't make a habit of living my life by the timeline of others.

I was traveling all over the United States, teaching and continuing my police work. After many months, I met Robyn towards the end of 2019 through mutual connections. We started talking while I was on the road, for hours and hours, about the important things in life, like core values and theology, as well as the unimportant things, like the things people do that annoy us! We both brought a "no-nonsense," fact-based approach to our conversations. Most men and women over the age of 35 will agree there isn't any room for games or false advertising when we're in the trenches of raising kids and careers. She was a private investigator, and we talked about our careers too. She has an alpha personality which is a great match for me because I tend to steamroll my way through things, and she quickly learned to balance that with her own equally-strong personality. She had to get used to the height adjustment since she's taller than me by a mile! I may be 5'3" with a seven-foot personality, but I'm still no match for her! When we got married, my bonus daughter Tori brought out a very strategi-cally-placed step stool so I could gain a few inches so I wouldn't have to hop up to kiss my bride!

As we got to know each other over the following four months, we made many trips between Mississippi and Louisiana. I would spend time with her kids in Louisiana, and she would come out to Mississippi to spend time with Kamran and establish a relationship with him. We took trips to see Mommy Lilly at the cemetery, and we would talk to Kamran about her. Robyn was great at guiding conversations and answering his questions as best she could, and certainly better than I ever could on my own. Questions like, "Where did she go? When will I see her? Why did she get sick? Why did she die?" You know, all the questions that no one can really answer perfectly for a little child. Robyn has an unwavering faith in God, and that's what she uses to guide her actions and her words.

In talking about God and Angels, she explained how he could think of Mommy Lilly as an Angel and that no matter what, she would always be a part of him. It wasn't long after that that Kamran became her "Angel Baby." It acknowledged Mommy Lilly, and at the same time, she got to call him *her* baby. Since then, it has been their special thing that bonds them in a unique way. His eyes light up when he's reminded that "Angel Baby" is HIS name only. After a collision of events on both of our ends, we mutually decided for Kamran to live with Robyn and her kids. The transition went better than I could have imag-ined. Robyn and her kids were excited to love on him, and I think he was so ready to be settled and loved on as well.

They welcomed him, and I'm so grateful for the love and care, and attention they showed and continue to show him. Robyn was not able to move, so I made the decision a few months later to officially move to Louisiana. I had been going back and forth as often as I could, but the travel was wearing on me. We found a house, and about two and a half years later, she finally said yes to marrying me! She knew I was not an easy man to live with but that I took my role seriously as the father, protector, and provider for our family.

Robyn has made countless sacrifices not only for Kamran but our family as a whole. She's made difficult decisions regarding her career in order to homeschool the boys Kamran and Tyler. She has turned a house into a home filled with love and positive influence because of the good, gracious, and godly woman that she is. Robyn has also created opportunities for Mommy Lilly to be part of Kamran's daily life, in the garden, in his bedroom when he wakes up and goes to sleep, as well as in our family room. Her selfless love has made Kamran feel so happy and secure, especially during his most influential years. She prays for us and with us, especially with Kamran, as she teaches him and raises him up.

Shawn Pardazi

After I moved to Louisiana, I had to decide what the next chapter would be in terms of my career. I decided to shift my focus to full-time teaching. I had already been teaching classes for the last ten years. Triple I Solutions had been my secondary source of income with my teaching career, and it became my full-time focus as the world headed into the Covid era.

As of writing this book, Robyn and I have just celebrated our first anniversary and going strong. Some say the first year of marriage is the hardest, but she says, and rightfully so, that the hardest year is the one that you are in. We don't know what the future holds, and as much as we try to plan it out, life has a funny way of taking those cards and throwing them up in the air, and letting them fall where they may.

It was a long and challenging mourning process after Lilly's passing, but I was fortunate in going through all that I did because it led me to finally find the woman that today is my Mrs. Robyn Pardazi. I have the best bonus kids, and she is the best mother to Kamran and loves him dearly. I couldn't have asked for a better partner, as she sets a positive example and takes such good care of all of us. We are thriving, and I'm so grateful for her.

Chapter 16
Stages of Jihad

In Western society, the term "Jihad" is typically a negative concept, but in actuality, it can be a very positive experience and process of growth and accomplishment. You have had stages of "Jihad" yourself; in your relationships, your financial struggles, education challenges, chronic illness, generational trauma, or simply struggles in your daily life. You may not be a Muslim, but you have most certainly had your own Jihad. Life is full of challenges, but your answer to your struggle IS your Jihad – it's the process of learning, stumbling, correcting your course, adjusting, receiving wisdom from others, and then reaching your goal or destination.

As a young boy, I began my life in Iran with a Jihad for the Iranian government. The mullahs had created a country where the purest of children were given a mission and purpose to serve a greater goal. Though my family kept me on the straight path, my spiritual journey began as a child and has stayed with me throughout my life. My religion is part of my ancestry and one I share with my son as he continues to carry on the title of Seyed. As I prepared to escape Iran, I embarked on a new Jihad. My mission and purpose became assimilation into the United States and the American way of life. It served as my freedom and saved my life. As I matured and answered the call to serve in law enforcement, my Jihad became the struggle of combating smuggling and terrorism, and also of survival. I taught others what I had learned to protect the greater community, my state, and the land I love.

As I embark on this next stage of life, writing this book has been its own Jihad. Organizing memories and words seems easy enough, but conveying the necessary emotions and scenarios can be challenging. I am experienced in my own field, but after publishing two books on my own, I have now included other talented people to help me to complete this special book. With the help of people with different strengths to overcome certain obstacles and challenges creates a more beneficial experience overall and an extraordinary result. My next Jihad is to pass the lessons and experiences on to others who come up the ranks. My struggles and experiences can help others overcome while becoming who they need to be in the process. This Jihad is also to provide for my family, set a positive example in raising my son to become a man of honor and integrity, be strong of body and mind, and pursue his ambitions and dreams—the American dream.

I attribute my success to the fact that I learned to communicate with people of all religions and cultures effectively, people who speak many different languages and have their own stories of immigration and assimilation. I became proficient in learning from all kinds of society as it shaped me as the "chameleon cop" to navigate different scenarios with people from various backgrounds. I also utilized the same skillset to continue teaching civilians, private corporations, and the intelligence community. To date, I have written and published two books, Evading Honesty and Smugglers, Inc.; both are available for the general public, the private sector, government agencies, and military branches. My latest and most recent course, *The Chameleon Cop,* was specifically designed for law enforcement to effectively communicate, de-escalate, properly evaluate, and objectively conduct investigations.

The only Jihad that may be out of reach is my height! Some things are God-given and here to stay. The only solution to remedy this is to buy boots to give me a couple more inches, which never hurt anybody!

As I wrap up this book, there is still religious and cultural conflict in the United States and around the world. Several months ago, there was a case in New Mexico where an Afghan Sunni Muslim committed a series of murders against Shiite Muslims. Sure enough, my phone began ringing as law enforcement colleagues wanted my opinion on the case. With a little research and asking a few of the right questions, I was able to determine a motive that no one else working on the case had considered. Local law enforcement doesn't always know the background of individuals in homicide cases. In this particular case, the man in question was upset that his daughter married a Shiite Muslim, so this was his method of retaliation. Acts of terrorism are still committed around the world. My training and education never cease, and my curiosity continues to inspire those who work alongside me to catch smugglers, identify terrorists, and make this country a safer place for all. The future of the United States can be a potentially bright one when it comes to matters of national security and protection of citizens. But as citizens, we must unite and combat the elements that hurt and destroy our society. These are citizens who want to live and provide for their families in the ultimate American dream. And I know the federal shad intelligence agencies are working diligently to understand the individuals and groups that wish to do us harm. My mission has been and will always be to grow as an educator and serve America to the best of my ability. I hope that in sharing my story with you, you were able to understand how someone with such a strong upbringing could grow into a loyal Patriot of the United States while maintaining a fondness for his beautiful homeland and some serious Chelo Kabob.

I salute you, the reader, for sharing this journey with me, for reading and learning what I hope has encouraged and entertained you and will help you elevate your personal journey and career.

About the Author

Capt. Shawn Pardazi is an internationally recognized speaker, author, and expert in the field of criminal and terrorism interdiction. During Shawn's 27-year tenure in law enforcement, he developed unique techniques and skillsets that enabled him to successfully identify and capture key assets of some of the world's most sophisticated smuggling operations.

Specializing in identifying clandestine activity, Capt. Pardazi developed a rapid assessment system to help identify OpSec countermeasures employed by clandestine operatives engaged in high-level smuggling operations. His language skills and his middle eastern background were utilized by numerous federal investigative agencies and international intelligence agencies around the world in HUMINT and other national security-related investigations.

Shawn has served in investigative capacities with the Federal Bureau of Investigation, DHS/Homeland Security Investigations, Internal Revenue Service-Criminal Investigations, and many other special investigative bodies and intelligence apparatuses within the United States and abroad. He continues to serve as a licensed law enforcement officer in three southern states in the United States. He is a certified police instructor in Texas as well as the US Department of Justice.

For more information, visit wwww.MyLETraining.com.

Also by Shawn Pardazi

For more information on any training, in-person events, online courses, or additional books by Shawn, visit www.MyLETraining.com.

www.ingramcontent.com/pod-product-compliance
Lightning Source LLC
Chambersburg PA
CBHW050524160726
48003CB00001B/443